AF657315

Practical Approach to Intellectual Property Rights

Practical Approach to Intellectual Property Rights

Rachna Singh Puri
CEO,
Xellect IP Solutions
Bangalore
Karnataka

Arvind Viswanathan
Chief Strategy Officer,
Xellect IP Solutions
Bangalore
Karnataka

I.K. International Publishing House Pvt. Ltd.

NEW DELHI • BANGALORE

Published by

I.K. International Publishing House Pvt. Ltd.
S-25, Green Park Extension
Uphaar Cinema Market
New Delhi – 110 016 (India)
E-mail: info@ikinternational.com
Website: www.ikbooks.com

ISBN 978-93-80026-69-5

© 2009 I.K. International Publishing House Pvt. Ltd.

Reprint 2013

All rights reserved. No part of this publication may be reproduced, stored in a retrieval system, or transmitted in any form or any means: electronic, mechanical, photocopying, recording, or otherwise, without the prior written permission from the publisher.

Published by Krishan Makhijani for I.K. International Publishing House Pvt. Ltd., S-25, Green Park Extension, Uphaar Cinema Market, New Delhi – 110 016 and Printed by Rekha Printers Pvt. Ltd., Okhla Industrial Area, Phase II, New Delhi – 110 020.

Dedicated to the creative force within each of us.

Preface

Intellectual Property results by virtue of an intellectual creation. Thus, everybody is potentially an owner of a piece of intellectual property in some form or the other. However, most often, the owner of an intellectual property is largely unaware of the nature of the intellectual property, and consequently, the manner in which to secure protection for it, and the value of the property as such. It is indeed a sad state of affairs that as human beings, we are all very rich in ingenuity and intellectual abilities, but remain poor due to our ignorance of matters related to intellectual property.

There are several types of intellectual property available to every individual or organization to be suitably leveraged for own gain. Any significant idea or intellectual creation can easily be classified into various facets of intellectual property. The first step involved after coming up with an idea is to understand which form(s) of intellectual property is most suited for it. Here, it must be understood that more than one form of intellectual property can be secured for a single idea.

Once the identification of the exact kind of intellectual property protection to be secured is made, the nature of presentation of the idea, the kind of information to be further obtained for it, the steps involved etc., will have to be delineated. This may be in the form of building prototypes, setting up experiments to obtain data to prove the concept, getting a high resolution drawing, and so on and so forth. The steps involved in securing the appropriate form of protection have not been very clear to a non-legal professional.

The authors have long recognized that the creators of intellectual property are non-legal professionals who excel in their respective fields, but have, so far, been forced to rely on legal professionals to secure the appropriate protection, and subsequent use of it. In this book, all forms of intellectual property have been described in a very simplistic manner to make it quite understandable to the creator of an intellectual property, such that the creator is capable of at the very least, identifying the form(s) of intellectual property most suitable for the creation. Subsequently, some insights as to how to secure the protection are also provided.

There is a greater emphasis on patents in this book, as patent is one of the most useful form of intellectual property for any technical ideas. There is a great deal of patenting activity all over the world, and India is very much in the forefront of this activity as well. However, in the authors' experience, there is a great amount of ignorance about patents, and even worse, a high level of misconceptions and wrong notions about patents. This book attempts to correct all such misguided thoughts and ideas about it, and to provide a clear guideline on what may be patented, how to obtain patent protection, and how best to use them after securing it.

The book also provides some insights on how to use the assets resulting from any intellectually creative endeavour. Securing protection for the intellectual effort may be a task unto itself, but it is only a first step towards achieving the goal of realizing its full value. All forms of intellectual property have a certain value in the commercial sense, and with a special emphasis on patents, some ways of arriving at the value are given. Some ideas on how best to assert one's rights once protection is secured is also given.

Each chapter in this book is a topic unto itself, and merits a book dedicated to it. The object of this book is to provide a simple introduction to each form of intellectual property, such that one uninitiated in the field of intellectual property can find out where one's intellectual creation fits best, and what is required to be done to secure the protection. This is in no way expected to replace the expertise of an experienced professional in the field, but provide some guidelines to seek the right kind of advice from the correct professional. Scientists, inventors, business managers, advisors, venture capitalists, and such professionals will find this text most useful in content and simplicity of presentation. Students interested in knowing more about this field so they can pursue their research and technology development better will also find this most compelling reading. Further, anyone interested in this field can ease into the field through this text, instead of burrowing through the heavy volumes that are otherwise offered.

AUTHORS

Foreword

After a lengthy, contentious and oftentimes tedious debate, on 1 January, 1995 India joined the World Trade Organization (WTO). In so doing, she acceded to an international legal instrument called TRIPs (Trade Related Intellectual Property Rights). This instrument linked India's continued access to international markets for her manufacturers and farm products to her taking steps to enshrine in law certain minimum standards of legal protection to be accorded to the owners of intellectual property – Indians and foreigners alike – against theft, misappropriation, unauthourised replication or fraudulent use.

TRIPs afforded India and other developing countries time till 1 January, 2000 to make their legal regimes governing intellectual property concordant with its requirements. Since 1999, not only has India amended then-extant laws, and enacted new ones, to fulfill her obligations under TRIPs, her parliament has seen it to be also to India's advantage to exceed in some of her laws on intellectual property the minimum requirements mandated by TRIPs.

If India is to gain from what her parliament has enabled, her creative people need to become aware of the opportunities afforded by the new legal regime governing their rights in the properties created by the exercise of their intellect, while being made alert to the pitfalls that accompany those opportunities. In this timely, handy and frustration-dissipating volume, Rachna Singh Puri and Arvind Viswanathan have assembled a portfolio of experience-based expert knowledge and legal acumen that can be relied upon by the creators of an invention or other forms of intellectual property to secure such robust legal protection for the products of their creative endeavours as will enable them to establish a profitable presence in the competitive global marketplace.

DR.V. SIDDHARTHA
Former Expert
Committee Established Pursuant
to United Nations Security Council Resolution 1540 (2004)
United Nations
&
Currently
Scientific Consultant (Advanced Technologies)
Office of the Principal
Scientific Adviser to the Government of India.
New Delhi.

Acknowledgements

There were various factors that inspired us to take up the project of coming out with a resource book on Intellectual Property Rights that is user friendly. For us one user was the 'creator' of any intellectual asset, another user was someone aspiring to become an 'IP Professional' and yet another user was the 'industry and business management' at large. Thus firstly we would like to acknowledge all such users who formed the inspirational core for our effort for this book, and hopefully who will benefit from reading this book.

This book would not have been possible without pitching in by other experts on select topics, and we wish to acknowledge the effort put in by these experts and thank them for so graciously working with us to give this book a wholesome approach. Malathi Lakshmikumaran and her team has always been a great support for us in all our initiatives and provides unique energy that fuels our ideas, R Saha who is a visionary and has several accomplishments to his credit on grass-root Government IPR initiatives, Vikrant Rana who is brilliant and is our resource bank for us on Trademarks, and Subodh Kumar who is leading several industry IPR initiatives and provided us great support to reach out to industry. We thank all these experts both in their individual capacity as friends and in their professional capacity as experts for joining hands with us on the journey of this book.

Our sincere thanks go out to several special people and organizations that have moulded and shaped us as professionals in general and as IP professionals in particular. Through my years of policy related grass-root work and working with Indian Industry on awareness campaigns at Confederation of Indian Industry (CII), I built a strong liking and foundation in this area. There are many special people in the CII team who were behind my success and who gently pushed me forward for greater responsibilities of representing the organization at World Intellectual Property Organization and other international forums. I wish to sincerely acknowledge the support and guidance of all my team members and my mentors during my enriching tenure at CII.

The grounding at CII helped me to take a leap to become the first member of the IP team at GE Global Research Centre at Bangalore, a team that stands to close to 100 IP professionals today. Excellent training, rigorous processes and a truly global environment at GE helped shape my skills in the Patent work area and gave me and Arvind tremendous insights of how critical IP is to a business. Our heartfelt thanks to all our mentors and peers in the IP work area both in India and abroad, who provided us the strong base for Intellectual Property and in the Patent field in particular.

I would also like to take this opportunity to thank my family who has shown tremendous patience as I chart my life path. It is difficult to express my gratitude in words for all the near and dear ones. Also, a word of thanks to special joy of my life, Siddharth, who makes everything I do so worthwhile.

Through this book we would like to share with the larger community our knowledge on the subject with a hope that Intellectual Property Rights is understood and used effectively for both individual and socio-economic gains.

AUTHORS

Contents

1

Introduction to Intellectual Property Rights

Intellectual Property Rights (IPR) are legal rights that may be obtained for any property that arises due to intellectual efforts of an individual or a group of individuals. Just like any other property, it can be bought, sold, traded, and licensed to others for use by its owner(s). To obtain the legal rights for intellectual creations, some basic procedures are to be followed. While the rights for intellectual creation may still belong to the owner, if the steps involved in procuring these rights are not adhered to, asserting the rights may become all the more difficult. Thus, obtaining protection for an intellectual creation is very important if one intends to obtain full value for the efforts expended.

In today's world, intellectual capital is considered to be a part of a company's assets and it is constantly assessed, valued, and even listed in the balance sheet. Intellectual capital of corporations results from accumulation of technical knowledge, patents, copyrights, tradenames or trademarks, brand values, etc. Intellectual capital is used extensively to procure bank loans, obtain funds from venture capitalists, enhance reputation and increase worth among shareholders, and build wealth.

IPR includes one among many different categories given below. In some instances, a creation may be protected under more than one form of IPR. The nature and form of protection for one's intellectual creation depends on the situation, and the law in effect in that jurisdiction (or country).

PATENTS

Patents are granted for an invention that stems from an idea that is novel, non-obvious and useful, and in many jurisdictions, must have industrial applicability. The idea presented should be complete in that one skilled in the same field as that of the invention, must be able to, upon reading the patent document, reproduce the invention as described. A patent, once granted in a particular jurisdiction, provides exclusivity rights from the state it was granted for a fixed period of time in exchange for a full disclosure of the invention.

There are several steps involved in filing a patent application, and subsequently, getting it granted. This will be addressed in the subsequent chapters in detail.

TRADEMARKS

Trademarks are distinctive signs used to denote goods or products. This is done in order to establish uniqueness of a product supplied by one company over all of similar or same products from other companies. Trademarks are usually a combination of one or more words, letters, signs, symbols, drawings, colours, 3-dimensional signs, and even smells. A trademarked goods is generally represented as the "name of the product" followed by the sign ™ e.g. TEFLON™ or the sign ® e.g. Xerox®.

Trademarks are registered with the respective trademark registration office. Registration of trademarks establishes assertion rights. The use of ™ does not automatically invoke any legal protection, but it is a very simple way of informing others that the sign or symbol or word, etc. is proprietary, and thus the inappropriate use of the same will be construed as infringement or counterfeiting, or both. The ® symbol is used when the trademark has been registered, while the ™ symbol may be used even before the registration.

Trademarks ensure that consumers can easily distinguish products, and enable companies to differentiate their products. Trademarks are increasingly being used for building brand image and reputation. Over the last couple of decades, the value of trademarks as an asset, and valuating them has become an important feature of any business.

Servicemarks are similar to trademarks, except that they are used to designate services instead of products. Servicemarks are represented as "name of service" followed by the symbol ℠.

Collective marks are marks used to distinguish goods or services produced or provided by members of an association. Collective marks are generally owned by an association or a cooperative. These are used when a group of enterprises find it to be a more effective way of marketing their products than if each of them attempts to market their products as individual marks.

Certification marks are used to distinguish goods or services that comply with a set of standards and have been certified by a certifying authority. An important point to note here is that the organization which provides these certification marks ought to be competent enough to certify any products or services.

Well-known marks are marks that have been in use in one or more regions and are considered to be well-known in those regions, as deemed by the competent authorities in the regions. Well-known marks enjoy strong protection despite not being registered with the appropriate authorities. However, establishing a symbol, sign, or word as a well-known mark is very time-consuming and easily susceptible to misuse by competitors while still in the stage of being established. It is generally used for long-standing marks that have been in use for a very long time.

COPYRIGHTS

Copyright is a form of intellectual property protection available to all forms of *expression* of ideas, procedures, methods of operation etc. It must be noted that copyright protection is available only to AN EXPRESSION of ideas, but not the ideas themselves. This form of protection extends to any form of expression, and includes, artistic, written, musical, movie form and so on.

Copyrights are automatic rights, in that the protection is obtained by virtue of creation by the copyright owner. Assertion rights are also automatically obtained, but getting the creation of work registered or witnessed by a third party with a date stamp facilitates assertion.

Software and algorithms are considered to be forms of expressions of ideas, and thus are protected by copyrights. However, software is constantly used in many technical fields to achieve various things. Thus, patenting of software has been debated, and the possibility has been explored, and is allowed by some countries with some caveats. But software assisted inventions are still hotly debated, and in many jurisdictions are not considered patentable. See Chapter 10 on page 67 Introduction to Patents.

TRADE SECRETS

Trade secret is the information that is deliberately kept a secret from public so that the secrecy invoked will provide an economic benefit or a competitive edge for the owner. To prove that the information kept secret is indeed a trade secret, reasonable efforts must be done to keep it out of reaching public attention, and ways of achieving it may include allowing access only to a select few, or locking it in a safe, the access to which is highly restricted.

A key difference between trade secret and other forms of intellectual property rights is that trade secret is the only one that is obtained by NOT disclosing the information to the public, whereas all other forms of protection is obtained by necessarily disclosing it.

GEOGRAPHICAL INDICATIONS

Geographical Indication (GI) is a sign used on goods that have a specific geographical origin or possess qualities or a reputation that are due to that place of origin. It is used most commonly for agricultural products whose qualities are influenced by specific local factors, such as climate and soil, but it is not necessarily restricted to agricultural products. A few examples include Tuscany Oil, Darjeeling Tea, Swiss Watches, etc.

INDUSTRIAL DESIGNS

Industrial designs are concerned with the aesthetic appearance of an article or a product. Industrial designs are also generally referred to as Designs. Designs are explicitly not concerned with any technical and/or functional considerations, but only the appearance. Appearance may include aesthetic or ornamental aspects of articles.

Appearance of an article or a product may manifest itself in the form of a two-dimensional feature, three-dimensional feature, shape of the product, surface finish of the product, patterns and colours on the surface of the product, and so on.

Ornamental or aesthetic appearances, covered under Designs, are generally known to increase visual appeal of a product. Designs, besides trademarks, are the first point of contact of any product with the consumer, and the first point of attraction. Any technical features may be used to attract the consumer later to buy a particular product over all the other existing similar products. Hence, Designs constitute an important form of intellectual property.

Designs are generally used for articles or products of "manufacture" only, whereas any single work of art will fall under the Copyright umbrella. Any kind of products, including products of handicraft manufacture, is susceptible to Design, and this may include disparate products such as watches, jewellery, automobiles, fans, lights, footwear, and so on.

PLANT VARIETIES

With the strong emergence of biotechnology and other related fields such as genetic engineering in the recent past, newer varieties of plants and animals are being produced. These animals and plants are largely similar to the existing varieties of animals and plants, but differ in some attributes as compared to the original. Such "designer" living beings are designed after considerable intellectual effort, followed by diligent experimentation in a laboratory. Hence, each jurisdiction needs to have adequate protection available to the person(s) investing time and resources into this effort.

Plant varieties are covered under a separate IPR system. Any new asexually reproduced new plant variety other than tuber propagated plant or plants found in uncultivated state may be protected under this IPR regime. It must be noted here that U.S. grants a Plant Patent, but this is not the same as a Utility Patent, but more akin to the Plant Varieties Protection.

The object of having an IPR system offering protection to plant varieties is to stimulate research and private plant breeding, enhance technology transfer, promote conservation of agro-biodiversity, among other things.

Despite U.S. granting a plant patent as early as 1931, and several countries discussing a system from the late-1950s, most countries took their time in assimilating this form of intellectual property into their overall IPR regime. India adopted it formally as the Protection of Plant Varieties and Farmers' Rights Act in 2000.

SEMICONDUCTOR INTEGRATED CIRCUITS LAYOUT DESIGN

Semiconductor Integrated Circuits or ICs have become an integral component in our everyday lives. They form part of every appliance that we use, which includes refrigerator, washing machine, computer, television, stereo system, etc. Since its first inception in the 1950s, ICs have had a tremendous impact in the progress of mankind.

The key feature of an IC is the presence of multiple circuits on a thin substrate. The substrate is typically made of a semiconductor material. ICs are very cheap to manufacture as compared to manufacturing individual circuits, and also show improved performance.

The design of Semiconductor Integrated Circuit Layout is protectable under a *sui generis* system. Typically, all ICs have a distinctive physical circuit layout in a large scale drawing. This drawing is used for manufacturing processes that may include steps of lithography, etching, coating, and others.

As any electronics engineer would attest, designing of ICs is an involved process that has to address several issues. All the circuits being combined have to function individually without being affected by the presence of the other. As is common in this field, miniaturization and increasing capacity is the name of the game. However, this comes with a price such as heating and consequent difficulty in heat management, and current leakage. A typical chip design has to address all the problems associated, and show improved performance over the existing chips. This requires considerable intellectual effort, and hence a suitable form of IPR was required.

U.S.A. was the first to introduce a suitable system for the protection of Semiconductor Integrated Circuits Layout Design in 1984, and several countries soon followed suit. Subsequently, agreement on Trade Related Aspects of Intellectual Property Rights (TRIPs) included a clause for all member countries to include a suitable IPR regime to provide for protection for Semiconductor Integrated Circuit Layout Design.

Under this form of IPR regime, any Integrated Circuit whose circuit layout is original, and the IC is for performing an electronic circuitry function can be protected by the appropriate registration. The IC must be inseparably formed on semiconductor or an insulator, and may also include layout of transistors and other circuitry elements, such as lead wires.

In subsequent chapters we will dig a little deeper into each of the above mentioned IPR forms to varying depths.

2

Copyrights

All of us have created something original on several occasions, perhaps even on a daily basis. The very act of speaking, writing, or even doodling is an act of possible creation of an intellectual property. The most relevant form of intellectual property towards any form of such expressions is copyright. As long as no copying of another's material is involved, the person who has written or doodled or drawn or recorded a speech is the owner of copyrighted material.

Having said this, the next level of detail that must be taken into account while discussing copyrights is when does this right arise? While as soon as some form of expression has occurred one has created copyrighted material, the rights associated with this form of intellectual property can be effectively enforced only on meeting the condition of reducing the expression into a tangible form. Reducing the expression to a tangible form means any form which is consistently reproducible without any loss during transfer. Such means may include written version, recordings on a medium like a cassette tape, a computer file, painted version on a canvas etc. Once this expression is affixed onto some tangible medium, then the creator of such material can confidently proclaim to the world that he or she is the owner of an intellectual property right and can also assert these rights.

WHAT DOES COPYRIGHT PROTECT?

Now, let us also examine this "expression" a little more carefully. Copyrights will protect the expression of ideas but not the ideas itself. This distinction must be clearly understood. As an example, consider a person standing on a mountaintop during sunset. This person becomes inspired by the sight and comes back to paint that image that is now affixed in her mind's eye. The sunset as seen from the mountaintop is the idea, while the painting is her expression. Copyrights can only be extended to the painting that was created, but not to the idea of the sunset itself. Any number of people can go to the same spot and become inspired by the same sight and create any number of versions of copyrighted material. Some may paint it all over again, others may describe it in prose, while some others may write poetry based on it, while a few may photograph it. And all of them will become legitimate copyright owners of their respective versions.

Similarly, let us take the example of a story plot line involving a love triangle. This plot line is the idea and forms the basis of several stories. Each story is the expression, which can be protected under copyrights, while the actual idea behind the stories cannot.

This concept can be extended to any situation, including a scientific situation. The basics of physics like the Newton's Law of Gravity or Einstein's Relationship between Energy and Mass are all ideas that cannot be protected or monopolized. All such laws belong to nature and are available to everyone. Further, copyright laws in almost all jurisdictions do not allow for the protection of mathematical formulae. But any creative ways of expressing these relationships, and explanations in words are all potentially copyrightable material. It must also be noted that simple explanation of the equation in words such as 'Energy is equal to the mass multiplied by the square of the speed of light' cannot also be copyrighted because it is the common way of explaining it.

Thus, publications of theories and concepts in peer reviewed journals or conferences are all copyrighted material, while the actual theories put forth cannot be monopolized. Indeed, as most of us who have published in the past already know, we do sign a copyright transfer form with the publisher of the journal prior to the publication of the paper. In a similar vein, all the graphs and tables providing scientific data are all protected under copyright, but the method used to obtain the data cannot be protected.

By the same token, software programs are immediately protected under copyrights. But, as mentioned earlier, the idea behind the software cannot be protected under copyright. Software is considered to be the expression of an idea in a tangible form. However, since it also has a technical effect in terms of executing some instructions to achieve a result, there is considerable debate as to providing protection through some other form of intellectual property, especially patents.

The copyright thus protects the form of expression of a creator against copying. The creators can expect a license fee for each copy of the original work. Copyright provides a bundle of rights including rights of reproduction, communication to the public, adaptation and translation of the work.

Like all other forms of Intellectual Property, Copyright has been internationally standardized, lasting between fifty to a hundred years from the author's death, or a finite period for anonymous or corporate authorship. Registration is not mandatory for copyrights and the mere act of creative expression in any medium awards the creator the copyright protection. Only the creator of such work or those deriving their rights through the creator can rightfully claim copyright.

RIGHTS GIVEN UNDER COPYRIGHT PROTECTION IN INDIA

Copyrighted works can be classified into various types of works:

Literary work
Dramatic work
Musical work
Artistic work
Sound recording, and
Cinematograph film.

Each of these kinds of work is associated with different rights as given below.

For literary work, copyright is the exclusive right to:

- Reproduce the work
- Issue copies of the work to the public
- Perform the work in public
- Communicate the work to the public
- Make cinematograph film or sound recording in respect of the work
- Make any translation of the work
- Make any adaptation of the work.

In addition to all the rights applicable to a literary work, owner of the copyright of a computer program enjoys the rights to sell or give on hire or offer for sale or hire, regardless of whether such a copy has been sold or given on hire on earlier occasion.

For dramatic work copyright is the exclusive right to:

- Reproduce the work
- Communicate the work to the public or perform the work in public
- Issue copies of the work to the public
- Include the work in any cinematograph film
- Make any adaptation of the work
- Make translation of the work.

For artistic work, copyright is the exclusive right to:

- Reproduce the work
- Communicate the work to the public
- Issue copies of the work to the public
- Include the work in any cinematograph film
- Make any adaptation of the work.

For musical work, copyright is the exclusive right to:

- Reproduce the work
- Issue copies of the work to the public
- Perform the work in public
- Communicate the work to the public
- Make cinematograph film or sound recording in respect of the work
- Make any translation of the work
- Make any adaptation of the work.

For cinematograph film, copyright is the exclusive right to:

- Make a copy of the film including a photograph of any image forming part thereof
- Sell or give on hire or offer for sale or hire a copy of the film
- Communicate the cinematograph film to the public.

For sound recording, copyright is the exclusive right to:

- Make any other sound recording embodying it
- Sell or give on hire, or offer for sale or hire, any copy of the sound recording
- Communicate the sound recording to the public.

Related Rights: Besides the rights in above classes, the Copyright Act provides protection in two special categories, **Performer's Rights** and **Broadcaster's Rights**.

Performer's Rights: As a performer, every individual has certain rights. These basic rights include the right to obtain some remuneration for one's work, and to obtain information about how one (including one's appearance) and other talents (acting, singing or other) may have been used in the final product. It includes the right to:

- Make a sound recording or visual recording of the performance;
- Reproduce the sound recording or visual recording of the performance;

- Broadcast the performance;
- Communicate the performance to the public otherwise than by broadcast.

Broadcaster's Rights: media broadcasters would have the right to protect the content of their media transmissions. Moreover, they would have the right to protect their broadcasts from reproduction, retransmission, and even from public communication. It includes the right to:

- Re-broadcast the broadcast;
- Cause the broadcast to be heard or seen by the public on payment of any charges;
- Make any sound recording or visual recording of the broadcast;
- Make any reproduction of such sound recording or visual recording where such initial recording was done without licence or, where it was licensed, for any purpose not envisaged by such licence; and sell or hire to the public, or offer for such sale or hire, any sound recording or visual recording of the broadcast.

INTERNATIONAL PROTECTION

As is the case, with all forms of Intellectual Property Rights, Copyright as provided by the Indian Copyright Act is valid only within the borders of our country. To secure protection to Indian works in foreign countries, India has become a member of the following international conventions on copyright and neighbouring (related) rights:

- Berne Convention for the Protection of Literary and Artistic works.
- Universal Copyright Convention.
- Convention for the Protection of Producers of Phonograms against Unauthorised Duplication of their Phonograms.
- Multilateral Convention for the Avoidance of Double Taxation of Copyright Royalties.
- Trade Related Aspects of Intellectual Property Rights (TRIPS) Agreement.

TERM OF COPYRIGHT

In India the copyright lasts for life of author or owner +60 years. In the case of cinematograph films, sound recordings, photographs, posthumous publications, anonymous and pseudonymous publications, works of government and works of international organisations, the 60-year period is counted from the date of publication. All terms of copyright generally run through the end of the calendar year in which they would otherwise expire, so a work enters the public domain on the first of the year following the expiration of its copyright term. For example, a book published on 29 April 1901 will enter the public domain on 1 January 1962, not 16 March 1961 (1901 + 60 = 1961).

The term for protection for Performer's Rights and Broadcaster's Rights is 25 years from the date of publication.

ADMINISTRATION OF COPYRIGHTS

The Copyright is administered under the Ministry of Human Resource and Development under the Central Government. An important development under the Copyright Act as amended in 1994, was the establishment of a Copyright Board. The Copyright Board is a deemed civil court and all the proceedings of the Board are deemed to be judicial proceedings.

REGISTRATION OF COPYRIGHT

As mentioned earlier, the very act of creating and fixing any expression gives the author or performer a copyright, because as per the Berne Convention, this right is an automatic right. Though it is not mandatory to apply for registration for copyright, however, the registration of copyright will serve as *prima facie* evidence in a court of law in any dispute relating to ownership of copyright. Registration will provide clear evidence of the manner and the text for which the copyright protection was sought and the date on which it was created. Thus, it is always advantageous to register any material to avoid any future disputes and to establish outright authorship.

The procedure for registration is set forth in Chapter VI of the Copyright Rules, 1956, and as amended, it includes:

- Application for registration is to be made on Form IV as prescribed in the first schedule to the Rules;
- Separate applications should be made for registration of each work;
- Each application should be accompanied by the requisite fee prescribed in the second schedule to the Rules; and
- The applications should be signed by the applicant or the advocate in whose favour a Power of Attorney has been executed. The Power of Attorney signed by the party and accepted by the advocate should also be enclosed.

It is important to note that both published and unpublished works can be registered.

- In case of published works, three copies of published work need to be submitted with the application.
- For unpublished work, two copies of the manuscript have to be submitted with the application.

The reason for submitting multiple copies is that one copy is used for affixing the stamp of the Copyright Office in proof of the work having been registered and is returned to the copyright owner and the other is retained in the Copyright Office for record and is kept confidential. For unpublished works, the applicant is also allowed to send only extracts from the unpublished work instead of the whole manuscript and ask for the return of the extracts after being stamped with the seal of the Copyright Office.

COPYRIGHT SOCIETY

A copyright society is formed by copyright owners for collective management and enforcement of their rights and is a registered collective administration society. As mentioned, the creators of copyrighted material as well as holders of related rights enjoy exclusive rights to authorise or prohibit the use of their works. However, enforcement by the rights holders' *vis-à-vis* individual members of the public may become very difficult, given the number and type of uses involved. In such cases, right holders are granted a remuneration right instead. These rights are typically managed by such societies.

A copyright society can issue or grant licences in respect of any work in which copyright subsists or in respect of any other right given by the Copyright Act. It can collect fees in pursuance of such licences and distribute such fees among owners of copyright after making deductions for the administrative expenses.

Ordinarily, only one society is registered to do business in respect of the same class of work. Some registered copyright societies in India are:

- **For cinematograph and television films**
  Society for Copyright Regulation of Indian Producers for Film and Television (SCRIPT) 135 Continental Building, Dr. A.B. Road, Worli, Mumbai-400 018.

- **For musical works**
  The Indian Performing Right Society Limited (IPRS), 208, Golden Chambers, 2nd Floor, New Andheri Link Road, Andheri (W), Mumbai-400 058.

- **For sound recordings**
  Phonographic Performance Limited (PPL) Flame Proof Equipment Building, B.39, Off New Link Road, Andheri (West), Mumbai-400 053.

COPYRIGHT INFRINGEMENT

Any violation of the rights conferred under the copyright to the owner of copyrighted works is deemed a act of infringement. These include:

- Making unauthorised copies for sale or hire or selling or letting them for hire;
- Permitting any place for the performance of works in public where such performance constitutes infringement of copyright;
- Distributing unauthorised copies for the purpose of trade or to such an extent so as to affect prejudicially the interest of the owner of copyright;
- Public exhibition of unauthorised copies by way of trade; and
- Import of unauthorised copies into India.

The remedies may be obtained by way of injunctions, damages and accounts. The concerned District Court has the jurisdiction in civil suits regarding copyright infringement. Additionally, all unauthorised copies of any work in which copyright subsists and all plates used or intended to be used for the production of such unauthorised copies are deemed to be the property of the owner of the copyright. The copyright infringement is a criminal offence under Section 63 of the Indian Copyright Act. A minimum punishment for infringement of copyright is imprisonment for six months with the minimum fine of Rs. 50,000/-. In the case of a second and subsequent conviction the minimum punishment is imprisonment for one year and fine of one lakh rupees.

FAIR USE

Use of copyrighted work without the permission of the owner is allowed in select instances including:

- For the purpose of research or private study,
- For criticism or review,
- For reporting current events,
- In connection with judicial proceeding,
- Performance by an amateur club or society if the performance is given to a non-paying audience, and
- The making of sound recordings of literary, dramatic or musical works under certain conditions.

The Fair Use concept is driven by a non-commercial angle and mostly applied for personal use or for educational purposes.

WORK FOR HIRE

The original holder of the copyright may be the employer of the author rather than the author himself, if the work is a "work for hire". For example, the Copyright, Designs and Patents Act, 1988 in England provides that if a copyrighted work is made by an employee in the course of that employment, the copyright is automatically owned by the employer as a "Work for Hire."

THE COPYRIGHT NOTICE

Some of the accepted copyright notices for visually perceptible copies contain the following three elements:

1. The symbol © (the letter C in a circle), or the word "Copyright," or the abbreviation "Copr."; and
2. The year of first publication of the work. In the case of compilations or derivative works incorporating previously published material, the year of first publication of the compilation or derivative work is sufficient. The year may be omitted where a pictorial, graphic, or sculptural work, with accompanying textual matter, if any, is reproduced in or on greeting cards, postcards, stationery, jewellery, dolls, toys, or any useful article; and
3. The name of the owner of copyright in the work, or an abbreviation by which the name can be recognized, or a generally known alternative designation of the owner.

   Example: © 2009 Rachna Singh

MORAL RIGHTS

Article 6bis of the Berne Convention is associated with the Moral Rights of any Copyrighted material, and states:

"Independent of the author's economic rights, and even after the transfer of the said rights, the author shall have the right to claim authorship of the work and to object to any distortion, mutilation or other modification of, or other derogatory action in relation to the said work, which would be prejudicial to the author's honor or reputation."

This clause is present to ensure that even after the author or the creator has assigned all the rights – including economic rights – to another entity, the author or creator still holds certain rights over the work. Thus, the current owner has some obligations towards the work that may include appropriate attributions such as naming the author. Furthermore, this work may also not be misused by the current owner to misrepresent the author.

Typically, moral rights are perpetual rights, and last forever, and in many countries the law states that explicitly. Moral rights cannot be assigned, but in many countries, such rights can be waived through the signing of appropriate contracts.

3

Trademarks

VIKRANT RANA
S.S. Rana Associates, Delhi

FUNCTIONS OF A TRADEMARK

A trademark indicates the source or origin of the product and helps in association of certain characteristics with the products or services. The concept of trademark is very important/valuable from the viewpoint of a consumer in a market with a number of competing suppliers providing essentially similar products. Trademark is the first point of contact for the company with the customer. The trademark applied by the manufacturer helps the consumer in making a choice by attaching a particular quality and source of origin to a product.

Trademark helps in distinguishing the trademark owner's goods and services from that of other traders. It helps in advertising as well. An important way to popularize a manufacturer's products is to popularize the trademark associated with it. It creates brand loyalty as customers associate a particular trademark with a particular product and ask for the product again and again if they are satisfied with the quality.

TRADEMARK SPECTRUM

Generic → Descriptive → Suggestive → Arbitrary → Invented
(Weakest)--(Strongest)

Generic trademarks are weak trademarks as the words defining the trademarks are generic to the trade and no one trader can have monopoly over the said mark, e.g. Reliable, Super, Best etc. Generic marks enjoy no legal protection.

Descriptive trademarks are also weak trademarks as they describe the goods and services, but they may qualify for registration upon proof of secondary significance i.e. an otherwise non-registrable trademark becomes distinctive, by virtue of continuous and extensive use over a period of time e.g. Real Juice, ROLLERBLADE etc.

Suggestive Trademarks are trademarks which are not "descriptive" but do indicate/suggest a connection with the product and services for which they are used. These trademarks evoke or suggest rather than describe. For example, although the trademark COPPERTONE does not describe any significant aspect of a suntan lotion, it does suggest the deep skin tone achievable through using the said lotion. Thus, COPPERTONE is considered a suggestive and therefore a strong trademark. Suggestive marks are powerful because they are memorable, create positive associations with the goods or services and can be registered without proof of the public's recognition of the mark. Another example of suggestive trademark is that of WHIRLPOOL washing machines.

Arbitrary trademarks are existing words used for goods and services, which bear no logical relationship to the goods and services for which the term is used. APPLE for computers was adapted because of the love of the co-founder of the Apple Inc. for the apples.

Invented Trademarks are invented words which are newly coined and had no meaning prior to their adoption, thus are distinctive and strong trademarks. For example, Kodak was adapted as a trademark because of its virtue of being a short name that cannot be mispronounced and that, it could not resemble or be with anything else. XEROX is an invented word derived from the Greek *xeros* (dry) and *graphos* (writing).

Arbitrary and Invented trademarks enjoy maximum legal protection but an intensive advertising campaign is required in order to make them popular, educate customers, trade as well as media.

Following are the different kinds of trademarks:

- An invented word or any arbitrary dictionary word or words, not being directly descriptive of the character or quality of the goods/services. e.g. Kellogg's.
- Any name (including personal or surname of the applicant or predecessor in business or the signature of the person), which is not unusual for trade to adopt as a mark, e.g. Saurav Ganguly, Tendulkar, TATA etc.
- Letters or numerals or any combination thereof: T of Tata, F of Ford, 007, 555, T20, 'M' of Mc Donalds Corporation
- Devices, including fancy devices or symbols: Nike Swoosh device

- Labels—Adidas
- Combination of colours or even a single colour in combination with a word or device: Standard Chartered Bank
- Shape of goods or their packaging: Toblerone Chocolate, Coca-Cola Bottle 
- In India, Yahoo Inc. has applied for the first sound mark registration (Yahoo Yodel). Sound marks when represented in conventional notation or described in words by being graphically represented can be registered
- Slogans: Just do it, Yeh dil mange more
- Characters—Cartoon characters: Fido Dido for 7'UP. Monster cartoon 
- In some countries, smell is also registered as trademark, e.g. smell of fresh grass applied to tyres.

ACQUISITION OF TRADEMARK RIGHTS

Registration of a trademark is not mandatory as rights in a mark accrue from the date of use. However, registration of a mark is advisable for its evidentiary value as well as statutory recognition. Registration gives a constructive notice to public at large and gives the owner an exclusive statutory right in respect of the goods and services for which it is registered. Registration is taken as a prima facie evidence of validity. In case of a registered trademark, infringement action can be taken against misuse of an unauthorised trademark rather than a passing off action. The onus in an infringement action is less as the plaintiff has to prove that he is the registered proprietor of the mark and the mark used by the defendant is similar to its mark.

Unregistered trademarks are protected under **Common law protection** in India. The honest prior user of a trademark can stop/prevent use by another party of the unauthorised mark, if damage is being done to his business by the use of the mark or by misrepresentation or confusion.

In contrast, **trademark registration** gives a **statutory right** to stop others from using the mark or a very similar mark for similar goods/ services in circumstances which could give rise to confusion or deception and which would be damaging to the reputation and goodwill of the registered proprietor. Trademark registration enables the owner of the mark to take the high ground against competitors who misappropriate the mark, or adopt something improperly close to it. In many cases, the trademark owner may even take action to stop the activities which may be perceived to be damaging as opposed to have really reached a stage at which they are actually damaging. Therefore, even though the registration is not mandatory, there are certain advantages of registration.

SELECTING A TRADEMARK

Important points to be remembered while selecting a trademark:

- A word mark should be easy to speak, spell, remember and recognize
- It should be distinctive
- Invented words or coined words are strong trademarks
- Laudatory word or words that describe the quality of goods (such as best, perfect, super etc.) should be avoided
- Descriptive words should be avoided
- It is advisable to conduct a market survey to ascertain if same/similar mark is used in the market
- A search be obtained from the Trademark Registry Office to ascertain if same/similar mark is registered or applied for registration
- In a growing global economy care should be taken to avoid linguistic traps, where a word/mark in one language may mean something else in a different language
- The trademark should not be identical or similar to the name of any company. To avoid this, name search can be conducted online at the website of the Ministry of Corporate Affairs (www.mca.gov.in)
- At the time of selection of a trademark, it is advisable to ascertain if the corresponding domain name for the trademark is available and if available, the said domain name may also be registered. Domain name availability can be ascertained for '.com', '.net', '.org', '.biz', '.info' domain names from 'whois database' at http://www.networksolutions.com/whois and for '.in', '.co.in' domain names from http://www.inregistry.in databases.

TRADEMARK REGISTRATION PROCEDURE IN INDIA

The Indian Trademark Act, 1999 defines a 'mark' to include, a device, brand heading, label, ticket, name, signature, word, letter, numeral, shape, packaging or conservation thereof.

Trademark search

Though obtaining a search report before filing an application is not mandatory, it is advisable as it would list all similar and identical trademarks registered and pending applications. This ensures that the time, money and efforts are not wasted in filing an application for a trademark which is already registered or subject of a pending application.

Information and documents required for filing a trademark application

For filing an application, following documents are required:

- Name, address and legal status of the applicant
- Whether manufacturer, merchant or service provider
- Date of first use in commerce in India or whether intent to use application
- Specifications of goods/services
- Classes of goods (India follows the 7th edition of the Nice classification i.e, it has 1 to 42 classes)
- Specimen of the mark
- Power of attorney
- Official fee of Rs. 2500 per class.

The Head Office of the Trademark Registry is at Mumbai, while the three branches are situated at New Delhi, Chennai, Ahmedabad. A person who claims to be the proprietor of a trademark can file application for registration of his trademark for goods and/or services with the appropriate office of the Trademark Registry under whose jurisdiction the principal place of the business or the address of the service of the applicant in India falls.

Examination

The Registrar may refuse or accept the application subject to the provisions of the Act. Grounds for refusal for registration of a mark are:

Absolute grounds for refusal

A trademark is refused registration under this category if:

1. It is devoid of any distinctive character; that is to say, not capable of distinguishing the goods or services of one person from those of others.
2. The trademark which consists exclusively of the marks or indications which may serve in trade to designate the kind, quality, quantity, intended purpose, values, geographical origins or the time of

production of the goods or rendering of the service or other characteristics of the goods or services.

The above categories of marks are registrable if they have acquired a distinctive character as a result of use or is a well known trademark.

Relative grounds for refusal

A trademark can be refused registration under the relative grounds of refusal if :

1. A mark is similar/identical to an earlier trademark for the same or similar goods/services.
2. A mark which is similar/identical to an earlier trademark in respect of different goods/services.

The above categories of marks may however be registered if the proprietor of the earlier trademark consents or there has been an honest concurrent use of the later mark.

Marks not registrable

This category includes marks which are not registrable under any circumstances. It is described as follows:

1. Trademark which is deceiving, confusing to the public or likely to hurt religious sentiments of any community or comprises any scandalous or obscene matter.
2. Trademark the use of which is prohibited under the Emblems and Names Act, 1950.
3. Trademark for the shape of goods which is purely functional or necessary to obtain technical result or which gives substantial value to the goods.

The objections raised by the Registrar with regard to an application are forwarded to the applicant and the applicant has to file an appropriate reply with the supporting documents to the official objections within one month. When an application for registration of a trademark is accepted, the Registrar advertises it in the official Trademarks Journal.

OPPOSITION TO A TRADEMARK

When a trademark is advertised in the Journal, any aggrieved person may within 3 months file notice of opposition against the said trademark. If no opposition is filed by any person within the statutory period, then the application proceeds to the registration.

TERM OF A TRADEMARK IN INDIA

Term of registration of a trademark is ten years, which may be renewed for a further period of ten years on payment of prescribed renewal fees.

Non-use of a registered trademark for a continuous period of five years is a ground for cancellation of registration of such trademark at the behest of any aggrieved party.

REMEDIES FOR PROTECTION OF TRADEMARKS

Remedies available for protection of trademarks are:

Civil Action – The competent courts can be moved for grant of relief against infringement and/or passing off.

Criminal Proceedings – Criminal complaints can also be filed against persons who have infringed the mark in addition to a civil action.

Administrative remedies – Notice of opposition can be filed against trademark application published in the Trademarks Journal. Proceedings can be initiated for rectification/cancellation of registered trademarks before the Registrar of Trademarks.

Companies Act: In addition to the above-mentioned remedies, action can be taken under Section 20 and 21 of the Companies Act in respect of a registered company which incorporates the trademark as part of its corporate name.

HOW NOT TO KILL YOUR TRADEMARK

It is important to note that the owners of once distinctive marks can lose protection by failing to police them. For example, Frederich Bayer & Co isolated acetylsalicylic acid in 1897 and branded it as 'Aspirin'. 'Aspirin' was registered as a trademark in Germany in 1899. After the First World War, other manufacturers began to sell identical products under the said name, which ultimately led to the mark's inability to identify a single source (i.e., Bayer). Therefore, the name no longer functioned as a trademark and 'aspirin' is now a generic term.

Further, it is important that the trademarks are used continuously as non-use of the trademark is a ground for cancellation. It is important to advertise trademarks rather than products: Trademarks should always be followed by a generic term: e.g. Wintex® tissue, Canon® camera, Eureka Forbes® vacuum cleaner, Bukhara® restaurant etc.

USAGE OF SYMBOLS ® AND ™ IN INDIA

Only the proprietor of a registered trademark can use the symbol ® in India. Using the symbol ® unless the mark has been registered is unlawful in India. Using symbol ™ with trademark simply means that one claims to be the proprietor of the trademark. There is no prohibition on the use of the symbol ™ in India.

4

Designs and Design Patents

What are the key factors to attract consumers to a particular product? You can think of any example of daily use. Let's look at an accessory like a 'watch' or a utility item like a 'refrigerator'. Besides the functional and cost aspects, another key factor that a consumer looks for is the visual appeal of all such items. Most of the advertising budget of companies focuses on the features that are visually appealing to a consumer. It could be a high-end product like Apple's iPod® or a desirable four or two wheeler or a container for a beverage like Coke®, Pepsi® or Thums-up®. The visual appeal of any article is embodied in its external design features or ornamentation. Indeed, consumers today are faced with products with almost same functions, but differentiated only in the visual appeal and the maker of the product. Thus, besides the brand name associated with the product, the visual appeal of a product is the most important feature that ensures greater sales in the marketplace.

Designs are commercially valuable and are applicable to a wide variety of products of industry and handicraft: from technical and medical instruments, watches, jewellery, footwear, home appliances, electrical appliances, vehicles, and many more items of industrial production.

Making products visually appealing without compromising their functionalities involves a heavy intellectual effort in itself. It is only fair to provide the creator of such visually appealing ornamental features some exclusivity rights for the efforts. The intellectual property right most appropriate for this is the Industrial Designs, or Design Patents in the U.S.A. Often times, Industrial Designs or Design Patents are generally referred to as simply 'Designs', and for convenience sake, throughout this text, we will refer to it also as Designs only.

WHAT DO DESIGNS COVER?

Under TRIPs (Trade Related Aspects of Intellectual Property Rights) Agreement under World Trade Organization (WTO), that lays the foundation for minimum standards for different Intellectual Property Rights, Articles 25 and 26 discuss Designs and mention that:

- Members to provide for the protection of independently created industrial designs that are new or original
- Members may provide that such protection SHALL NOT EXTEND TO DESIGNS dictated essentially by technical or functional considerations
- Members to grant the owner of a protected industrial design the right to prevent third parties not having the owner's consent for making, selling or importing articles bearing or embodying a design which is a copy, or substantially a copy, of the protected design, when such acts are undertaken for commercial purposes
- The duration of protection available shall amount to at least 10 years.

The guidelines for protection of Designs at an international level are governed by the Hague Agreement administered by World Intellectual Property Organization (WIPO) that covers the protection for Designs and international registration of the same.

Thus, to reiterate, Designs in context of intellectual property refer to the ornamental or aesthetic aspect of an article that increases the visual appeal of the article. These may include three-dimensional features, such as the shape or surface of an article, or of two-dimensional features, such as patterns, lines or colour.

Now let's see how does the protection offered for Designs differ from that by Patents or Copyrights.

DESIGNS VS PATENTS

Broadly "patent or utility patent" protects the way an article is used and works, while "Design", "Industrial Design" or "Design patent" protects the way an article looks. Both design and utility patents may be obtained independently on an article if novelties in the article reside both in its utility and ornamental appearance.

DESIGN VS COPYRIGHTS

Designs are applicable to articles capable of "manufacture" i.e. Industrial Applicability is required whereas Copyrights are for works of art and generally not mass-produced, except books, movies etc.

INDIAN DESIGN ACT, 2000

Under the Indian Design Act, 2000, 'Design' covers the features of shape, configuration, pattern or ornament or composition of lines or colour or combination. It can be applied to any article whether two dimensional or three dimensional.

It should be made by any industrial process:

- Manual
- Mechanical
- Chemical or
- Combined.

Under the Indian Industrial Design Act, following are not registrable:

- Any mode or principle or construction or anything which is in substance a mere mechanical device.
- Any trademark, property mark or artistic work.
- Normally, designs of artistic nature like painting, sculptures and the like which are not produced in bulk by any industrial process are excluded from registration under the Act. Such artistic works not amenable to industrial processes are covered under Copyright Act.
- Designs of industrial plans, layouts and installations.
- Book jackets, certificates, forms, calendars and other documents, dress making patterns, greeting cards, leaflets, maps and playing cards, postcards, stamps, medals, labels, tokens, cartoons, flags, emblems of countries.
- Layout designs of integrated circuits.
- Material that contains or comprises matter of scandalous or obscene nature.
- Material that is contrary to public order or morality.

As explained before, Designs are obtained for any aesthetic designs of an article. The underlying meaning of this statement is that once this aesthetic design is removed, an article must remain behind. As an illustration, consider a bottle, on to which you wish to have some ornamental engravings made to attract the consumers' eye. Once these engravings are removed, a bottle still remains behind in principle. As a further illustration, a Design protection can also be obtained for designs of patterns on clothes. In this situation, if the patterns are removed, an article viz. the cloth still exists.

CLASSIFICATION OF DESIGNS

The internationally harmonized scheme of classification was formally adopted by several countries at a diplomatic conference held in Locarno, Switzerland on October 8, 1968. The agreement is referred to as Locarno Agreement Establishing an International Classification for Industrial Designs, and the classification system is called Locarno Classification. All the Designs applied for and granted are classified in principle, first according to their purpose and subsidiarily, according to the object that they represent. This latter classification is optional. As of January 1, 2009, 49 countries, and four organizations (such as ARIPO) were party to the Locarno Agreement, and have adopted and applied the Locarno Classification for Industrial Designs. India also uses the International Classification based on Locarno Classification.

Under the Locarno Classification system, there are 32 Classes and 219 sub-classes containing over 7000 listing of different goods. For example, Class 1 relates to foodstuff, Class 6 relates to furnishings, class 8 relates to tools and hardware, class 24 relates to medical and laboratory equipment and so on. (See: http://www.wipo.int/classifications/nivilo/locarno/index.htm#)

Elements of Industrial Design Act, 2000 include:

- Design should be new or original, not previously published or used in any country before the date of application for registration.
- Novelty may reside in the application of a known shape or pattern to new subject matter.
- Design should be applied or applicable to any article by any industrial process.
- Design must appear and should be visible on the finished article, for which it is meant.

It is important to note, and certainly worth reiterating, that the article for which the Design is being registered must have its existence independent of the Designs applied to it. If on removing ornamentation only a piece of paper, metal or like material remains and the article referred to ceases to exist then the design is not registrable.

WHO CAN APPLY FOR REGISTRATION OF A DESIGN?

Any person who has created a design can file for registration of the Design. An application may also be filed in the name of the company, regardless of whether the company is a firm, partnership or a corporate entity. Further, the application can also be made by a legal representative of the person or a company. Typically, a legal representative is one who has passed the patent agent examination, and is listed as an active patent agent.

SEARCHING AND ENSURING NOVELTY OR ORIGINALITY OF DESIGN

Any Design can be checked for its novelty or originality by appropriately petitioning the Design Office along with the fees. The Office will submit a report based on its search to the applicant. The search report can be used to one's advantage to ensure that the Design created is indeed new or original. If the search report happens to be less than satisfactory towards the applicant, then the applicant has been saved from potential danger of infringement of another's registered Design.

HOW TO APPLY FOR A DESIGN REGISTRATION

For registering a Design with the Patent, Trademark and Design Office in India, some of the key requirements for the paperwork include:

Form-1: The form should contain several details, some of which are name in full, address of the person or the organization, address for service in India (if different from the address of the organization/person), nationality, name of the article, class number. The application needs to be signed either by the applicant or by the authorized agent.

Drawings: Drawings are the most important element of a Design application. Typically, either a drawing or a black and white photograph of the claimed design is acceptable. It is best to include a sufficient number of views (4 copies of the drawings are needed). Good drawings will ensure complete disclosure of the appearance of the claimed design. For the drawings, perspective views are most desirable. There is no need to illustrate hidden parts or sectional views or exploded views. No dimensions or engineering symbols are needed. No text matter or reference numerals are to be used other than to indicate the novel aspects.

A Statement of Novelty should be submitted for the Design Application and it:

- defines the design which applicant wishes to register, in terms of the article in which it is embodied or applied;
- must be in formal terms that addresses "The ornamental design for (the article which embodies the design or to which it is applied) as shown or as shown and described."

Some examples for the statement of novelty are:

"Novelty resides in the shape and configuration of the article shown in FIG...."
"Novelty resides in portion X of the illustration".
"Novelty resides in the ornamentation or surface pattern of the article."

Like in all other filing procedures, if the application is filed through an agent, a separate power of attorney needs to be filed, which states that the concerned agent is authorized to represent them for the Design registration.

If the ornamental pattern can be confused with a trademark, a disclaimer to this regard is specifically needed. Similarly disclaimers are needed for any associated mechanical action or use of words, numerals and letters.

If the registration has been filed in any country outside India, the applicant can claim priority of that date but the subsequent filing in India must be within 6 months of any foreign filing.

EXAMINATION TIMELINES

The application is given a number in the order of its receipt and the date of the application is the actual date of its receipt in the office. Defects in the application, if any noticed on examination of the application are communicated to the applicant or to the authorized agent at the address for service. The defects should be corrected and the application resubmitted to the Design office for acceptance WITHIN SIX MONTHS FROM THE OFFICIAL DATE OF THE APPLICATION. Within 6 months of date of application, if neither a petition for extension is filed by the applicant nor the time period is extended by the Controller, the application will be examined, and a decision as to whether it is granted or rejected will be made. The applicant will be notified as to the decision.

Any decisions made by the Controller may be appealed by the applicant within three months of the date of the decision.

Following the grant of a Design, it is published in the gazette which is available for public inspection. Any interested parties are allowed to inspect the gazette and provide objections to the registration of a Design at any time after the registration by filing a petition to the controller. There are specific grounds upon which objection for registration can be raised, which includes reasons like the Design is not new or novel, or has been registered previously in India, or published anywhere in the world.

U.S. offers a Design Patent for ornamental features of a functional item. In US new text fonts and computer icons are also covered by the design patents. As a matter of fact, the first design Patent was for a font. Interestingly, the Statute of Liberty was also covered by a design patent.

TERM OF PROTECTION

In India, a Design registration lasts for a period of 10 years. Further, before the expiry of the 10 year period, a petition for extension may be filed to extend the protection for another 5 year period. Thus, the maximum lifetime a Design enjoys is a total of 15 years.

In the U.S., a Design lasts for a maximum period of 14 years, while in Japan, the life of a Design is 15 years. In the Office for Harmonization of Internal Market for Trademarks and Designs, which is the trademark and industrial designs registry for the internal market of the European Union, the Design protection lasts for a maximum of 25 years. However, this term is subject to the payment of renewal fees every five years.

In Europe, both registered and unregistered Community designs are allowed which provide a unitary right covering the European Community. The unregistered Community design lasts for three years after a design is made available to the public. National systems of registered designs exist alongside the system of Community designs. The criteria for eligibility and the duration of protection are the same as for registered Community designs.

DESIGN INFRINGEMENT

In India—use of a registered design or its imitation to any article belonging to class of articles in which the design has been registered for the purpose of sale or import of such articles without the written consent of the registered proprietor is considered infringement. Monetary damages are available for design infringement. The suit for infringement, recovery of damage etc., should not be filed in any court below the court of District Judge.

In US—not exact copy of the Design but even substantially similar is considered infringement. Publishing such articles or exposing terms for sale with knowledge of the unauthorized application of the design to them also involves piracy of the design.

In Europe—infringement is said to occur only if the protected design has been exactly copied.

Designs are an extremely important form of intellectual property, in that they are the very essence of taking a functional item and making it visually appealing, thus making it attractive in the marketplace. It is now understood that it was an extremely well thought-out design, and protected with exclusivity rights, that made IPod® the successful product as we know it. Action figures and toy items such as Darth Vader, Luke Skywalker, and Transformers were all protected under Designs.

"When I'm working on a problem, I never think about beauty. I think of only how to solve the problem. But when I have finished, if the solution is not beautiful, I know it is wrong." —R. Buckminster Fuller.

5

Semiconductor Integrated Circuits and Layout Designs

Semiconductor Integrated circuits, also known as Integrated Circuits or ICs form the backbone of all electronic devices available today. Integrated circuits are miniaturized electronic devices in which a number of active and passive circuit elements are located on or within a continuous body of material to perform the function of a complete circuit. The term "integrated circuit" is often used interchangeably with such terms as microchip, silicon chip, semiconductor chip, and micro-electronic device. Microprocessor is just one kind of an Integrated Circuit, the Random Access Memory (RAM) is another kind of Integrated circuit. There are several such integrated circuits in all computers and electronic devices and even in consumer durables like refrigerators, television, cellular phones etc.

Integrated circuits have a distinctive physical circuit layout, which is first produced in the form of a large scale drawing and later reduced and reproduced in a solid medium by high precision electrochemical processes. The layout of an integrated circuit includes one or more cross-sectional drawings which are superimposed upon each other and which together represent the complete integrated circuit or complete topography. The term "topography" describes a three-dimensional, layered "hill and valley" configuration which embodies the miniature electronic circuits of an integrated circuit.

The design of ICs involves considerable intellectual effort. Several parameters have to be taken into consideration while designing, and the final IC as envisioned has to perform at its optimal best. To ensure the chip as designed is performing at its best, considerable amount of time and resources had to be expended. It was estimated by chip manufacturers that designing a single IC may cost anywhere upwards of USD 100,000.

However, once a chip has been designed, it is quite simple to copy the design. The chip manufacturers estimate was that it costs less than USD 10,000 to copy an original design that cost almost ten times more to arrive at. Copying could be achieved through several means, e.g. photographing each layer of an integrated circuit.

In the early days of chip design and manufacturing, "chip graffiti" was the more prevalent method to thwart illegal copying. Thus, if someone attempted to steal the chip design by simply copying the masks, it would be necessary to copy the graffiti also, which would expose the fraudulence involved. Graffiti was so necessary to prove illegal copying as just showing that the rest of the mask was identical was not sufficient proof of copying. However, this was still not a very strong method for protection, as the very act of coming up with graffiti became a tedious effort, and rather wasted in the bigger scheme of things. In 1984, the U.S. Congress passed the Semiconductor Chip Protection Act to protect IC Layout by a *sui generis* system. After this, an identical copy of a mask's working parts was an automatic copyright violation, and so graffiti served no useful purpose.

To protect the efforts for developing IC Layout Design, presently more than 20 countries have put some kind of legislation to protect IC layout. Japan enacted the Japanese "Act Concerning the Circuit Layout of a Semiconductor Integrated Circuit" of 1985. In 1986 the EC promulgated a directive requiring its members to adopt national legislation for the protection of semiconductor topographies via Council Directive 1987/54/EEC of 16 Dec 1986 on the Legal Protection of Topographies of Semiconductor Products. In the TRIPs Agreement Part II, section 6 deals with semiconductor chip products. An Intellectual Property in Respect of Integrated Circuits (IPIC) Treaty was proposed in the Diplomatic Conference in Washington D.C. in 1989 and the TRIPs Agreement incorporated the IPIC Treaty by reference with modifications under Article 35 of TRIPs.

IC LAYOUT PROTECTION IN INDIA

A *sui generis* (meaning "one of its kind") system for protection for semiconductor IC layout designs is available in some countries like India. The Indian legislation for IC layout designs is covered by the Semiconductor Integrated Circuits Layout Design Act, 2000 (Hereinafter, this will be referred to as SICLD Act, 2000) and comes under the purview of DIT, Ministry of Communications & Information Technology.

Definitions

Some basic definitions under the Indian Act include:

"Layout-design" means a layout of transistors and other circuitry elements and includes lead wires connecting such elements and expressed in any manner in a semiconductor integrated circuit.

"Semiconductor Integrated Circuit" means a product having transistors and other circuitry elements which are inseparably formed on a semiconductor material or an insulating material or inside the semiconductor material and designed to perform an electronic circuitry function.

Criteria for Registering IC Layout Designs

According to Section 7, paragraph 2 of the SICLD Act, 2000, a layout-design shall be considered to be original if it is the result of its creator's own intellectual efforts and is not commonly known to the creators of layout-designs and manufacturers of semiconductor integrated circuits at the time of its creation. For registering the IC Layout Design, some salient features under this Act include that the layout design:

- must be original
- should not have been already commercially exploited anywhere in India or in a convention country
- must be inherently distinctive
- must be inherently capable of being distinguishable from any other registered layout design
- must be inseparably formed on a material that is semiconducting or insulating
- may also be inside the material
- is for performing an electronic circuitry function
- includes layout of transistors and other circuitry elements, and even lead wires connecting such elements
- covers any manner of expression in a semiconductor IC.

It must be understood that only the IC Layout Design, which in essence is the "floor planning" of the integrated circuits can be registered under the SICLD Act, 2000. Other types of information such as the ideas behind it, procedures, processes, systems, program stored in the integrated circuit, methods of operation etc., cannot be protected under this Act.

In case the layout design has been commercially exploited, a grace period of two years is provided for registration within which the applicant can register for the design in India or in a convention country.

Further, Section 7, paragraph 3 of the SICLD Act, 2000 states that where an original layout-design has been created in execution of *a commission or a contract of employment*, the right of registration to such layout-design under this Act shall belong, in the absence of any contractual provision to the contrary, *to the person who commissioned* the work or to the *employer*.

Who can apply under the Indian Act

The creator of an IC Layout Design is given the opportunity to file and procure the rights to the creation. Considering the time, effort and knowledge required to put together the paper work (as with all intellectual property rights and indeed all legal-related matters), any legal practitioner can apply on behalf of the creator. Further, there are persons registered as layout-design agents who can act on behalf of the creator also. These layout-design agents are the IC Layout Design equivalents of Patent Agents or Trademark Agents. Also, any authorized person in the sole and regular employment of the organization associated with the IC Layout Design can also file in the name of the organization.

How to Apply for the Registration of an IC Layout Design

The application for registration of an IC Layout Design typically comprises a Form LD-1, the prescribed fees (which as of January, 2009 is INR 5,000/-), 3 sets of drawings which adequately describes the IC layout design, 3 sets of photographs or drawings of masks used for the fabrication of the semiconductor IC. Any written description associated with the IC Layout Design may also be included in the registration paperwork.

Post-Application Process

If the Registrar of the Semiconductor IC Layout Design is convinced that the application for an IC Layout Design cannot be registered, the Registrar will inform the applicant about it, along with the reasons for the conclusion. The applicant is allowed to present his version of the same case. Even after the hearing of the applicant's version, if the Registrar is not convinced about the strength of the applicant's position towards the IC Layout Design, then the Registrar will proceed to reject the application.

However, if the Registrar is convinced that the IC Layout Design is indeed registrable, or is convinced upon hearing the applicant's arguments, then the Registrar will notify about the acceptance and proceed to publish it in the gazette.

Section 13 of the SICLD Act, 2000 also states that "Where registration of a layout-design is not completed within twelve months from the date of the application by reason of default on the part of the applicant, the Registrar may, after giving notice to the applicant in the prescribed manner, treat the application as abandoned." This essentially states that any oversight on the part of the applicant will result in the abandonment of the application.

Opposition Proceedings

After the registration of an IC Layout Design, and publication in the prescribed manner, any person may oppose to the registration by giving notice in writing in the prescribed manner to the Registrar within three months along with the prescribed fee. The Registrar then proceeds to notify the applicant regarding this opposition within two months from the date of receipt of the notification of opposition. The applicant is given full opportunity to provide a counter-statement to rebut the opposition. Failure to respond results in the abandonment of the application. The counter-statement by the applicant will be sent to the person opposing the registration. Thus, this process continues, which may even include a hearing, wherein the two parties are allowed to sit across a table in the presence of a mediator – usually the Registrar or a suitable representative – until the case is resolved.

Rights Conferred upon Registration of an IC Layout Design

Once an IC Layout Design has been registered, then this confers upon the applicant the right to use, distribute, import (affirmative right unlike Patents) the IC using the design, and prohibits unauthorized reproduction of the chip incorporating the IC Layout Design and importing or selling or otherwise distributing for commercial purposes. This encompasses not only a registered layout-design, but also a semiconductor IC incorporating the layout-design, and an article incorporating the semiconductor IC having the layout-design.

However, if any act of reproducing or importing or such are performed for the limited purposes of scientific evaluation, analysis, research or teaching, then this act does NOT constitute as an act of infringement.

Also, the exclusive right of an applicant to "use" a registered IC Layout Design does not prohibit an independently created mask work of identical geometry (which right is similar to copyrights). Furthermore, reproduction for reverse engineering of a mask work is specifically permitted by the law. As with copyright, mask work rights exist when they are created, regardless of registration, unlike patents, which only confer rights after application, examination and issuance.

Once registered, the Proprietor can take any action on the layout-design. The layout-design can be assigned or transmitted to another. Any person who applies for and obtains permission to use the layout-design is referred to as "Registered User". All assignments must be done in a prescribed manner to the Registrar and must also be accompanied by the agreement in writing or a duly authenticated copy thereof an affidavit giving particulars of the relationship showing degree of control, term of relationship, any conditions or restrictions. Such information will be listed in the Registry. A registered user, as long as he is listed as one, can act as if he were the proprietor, except the assigning or transmission rights.

Term of Protection of IC Layout Designs in India

Most countries including India have a 10-year period of protection for IC Layout Design.

Infringement of Rights Conferred

An act of infringement is said to have occurred if one without permission does any act of reproducing, importing, selling or otherwise distributing for commercial purposes a registered IC Layout Design. As mentioned earlier, since the rights extend not only to the registered IC Layout Design, but also to semiconductor IC incorporating the IC Layout Design, and an article incorporating the semiconductor IC Layout Design. Hence, committing any act of reproducing, importing, selling or otherwise distributing for commercial purposes even a semiconductor IC incorporating the IC Layout Design or an article comprising the semiconductor also constitutes an act of infringement.

Any act of infringement done knowingly and willfully shall be punishable with either imprisonment upto three years, or fine not less than INR 50,000 upto INR 10 lakhs, or both.

Proper Representations of Registered IC Layout Designs

There are serious implications of using the word "Registered" for semiconductor Integrated Circuit layout design. If the word "Registered" in reference to the IC Layout Design is used in another context then it should clearly state so and the other characters must be at least as large as those in which that word is delineated. A penalty for falsely representing an IC Layout Design as registered will incur imprisonment upto six months, or fine upto INR 50,000, or both.

6

Protection of Plant Varieties and Farmers' Rights

MALATHI LAKSHMIKUMARAN
Lakshmikumaran & Sridharan, Delhi

TRIPs—ARTICLE 27

Article 27, Article 28, Article 29 and Article 30 are relevant for the Intellectual Property Rights related to patents. Further, Article 27(3)(b) of the TRIPs Agreement which is the basis of most patent law in the world today states:

> "Members may also exclude from patentability.... Plants and animals other than micro-organisms, and essentially biological processes for the production of plants and animals other than non-biological and micro-biological processes. However, Members shall provide for the protection of plant varieties either by patents or by an effective *sui generis* system or by any combination thereof."

As is seen, Article 27(3)(b) of the TRIPs Agreement states that plants and animals other than micro-organisms, and the processes for producing them shall not be patentable, but, the Member States shall provide a *sui generis* system or an alternate form of protection or patent protection or a combination of both to safeguard the new varieties evolved as a result of genetic modification.

PROTECTING PLANT RELATED DEVELOPMENTS

United States

In the U.S., there are three forms of protection for plant related inventions. These are Utility Patents, Plant Patent Act (PPA), Plant Variety Protection (PVP). The utility patents and the plant protection patents are granted by United States Patent and Trademark Office (USPTO) while the PVP is granted by Plant Variety Protection Office governed by United States Department of Agriculture (USDA). Utility patents awarded in U.S, cover conventionally bred varieties or genetically modified plants.

Plant patent is a right granted by the Government to an inventor who has invented or discovered and asexually reproduced new plant variety other than tuber propagated plant or plant found in uncultivated state.

A sport or mutant of a patented plant is not considered to have same genotype as that of the parent plant. Hence, such plants are separately patented instead of being covered by the plant patent of the parent plant.

The first plant patent was issued in 1931 to Henry Bosenberg of New Brunswick, NJ for a climbing or trailing rose. This invention was for climbing roses bearing true blooming character. There was another plant patent for a rose plant named 'Breapum' granted to Ezio Brea in 2003 (USPP14, 226 P3). The new and distinct cultivar had the unique characteristics of long erect flowering stems, creamy white coloured flowers and orange coloured hips arranged in sprays. A patent for Chrysanthemum plant named 'Zembla' (US PP14, 052 P2) was granted which was for an invention distinct in possessing decorative inflorescence and possessing excellent post-production longevity.

India

Under Section 3(j) of Indian Patents Act, 1970 plants are not considered patentable subject matter. Under Section 3(h) of the Act, methods of agriculture and horticulture are not patentable. Similarly, essentially biological processes for the production or propagation of plants are not patentable under section 3(j) of the Indian Patents Act, 1970. Plant varieties may be protected in India under Plant Varieties Protection and Farmers' Rights Act (PVPFRA), 2002, a *sui generis* system. The major objectives of this Act are to stimulate research and private plant breeding, enhance technology transfer, foreign investment and trade, promote conservation of agro biodiversity and sustained use of varieties and facilitate access to genetic resources and sharing benefits.

Registration of new plant varieties

(1) A new variety shall be registered under this Act if it conforms to the criteria of novelty and fulfills the *DUS Test*. DUS stands for distinctiveness, uniformity and stability.

   (a) **Novelty**—the variety should not have been sold (offered for sale) or marketed earlier than one year for the country and four years for other countries where protection is desired. (In the case of trees and vines it is six years.)
   (b) **Distinctiveness**—the variety should be clearly distinguishable from any other variety of common knowledge.
   (c) **Uniformity**—variety is uniform/homogeneous if, subject to the variation that may be expected from the particular features of it's propagation, it is sufficiently uniform in its relevant characteristics.
   (d) **Stability**—variety is stable if its relevant (essential) characteristics remain unchanged after repeated propagation or, in the case of a particular cycle of propagation or, in the case of a particular cycle of propagation, at the end of each cycle.

(2) No variety shall be registered under this Act if it contains any gene or gene sequences involving any technology including terminator technology which is injurious to the life or health of human beings, animals or plants.

FARMERS' RIGHTS

In case of International Union for the Protection of New Varieties of Plants (UPOV) 1991, the farmer's right to save the seeds for subsequent use is actually forbidden and is conditional upon 'legitimate' interests of the breeders', i.e. the royalty that should be paid to the breeder. The Indian PVP Act differs in this aspect as it allows the farmers' privilege, since it explicitly recognizes community and farmers rights by including a specific clause on the subject. Nothing shall affect the right of a farmer to save, use, exchange, share or sell his farm produce of a protected variety except in case where the sale is for the purpose of reproduction under commercial marketing arrangement. The Farmers' rights also include the rights arising from conserving, improving and making available the genetic resources.

RESEARCHERS' RIGHTS

A free access to protected varieties for conducing experiments or for bonafide research purposes to create other varieties is allowed. Authorization of breeder will be needed for repeated use of protected variety as a parental material for commercial production or marketing arrangement.

RIGHTS OF COMMUNITIES

Any person/organization may stake a claim on behalf of a village or local community in regard to the contribution of that village or local community in the evolution of a variety. Compensation may be granted by PVP authority for their contribution in evolution of a new variety. Sharing of benefits accruing to a breeder is provided for in case of a variety that is developed from indigenously derived plant genetic resources (of governmental institutions, non-governmental organizations, private breeders, village and tribal communities).

ESSENTIALLY DERIVED VARIETY

In respect of a variety (in this clause to be called "the initial variety"), an 'essentially derived variety' shall be said to be essentially derived from each initial variety when it:

(i) is predominantly derived from such initial variety, while retaining the expression of the essential characteristics that result from the genotype or combination of genotypes of such initial variety;
(ii) is clearly distinguishable from such initial variety; and
(iii) conforms to such initial variety in the expression of the essential characteristics that result from the genotype or combination of genotypes of such initial variety except variation in such characteristics which result in the process of derivation.

WHO CAN FILE?

Any person claiming to be the breeder of the variety; or his/her successor or assignee; or any farmer or group of farmers or community of farmers claiming to be the breeder of the variety; or any university or publicly funded agricultural institution claiming to be the breeder of the variety is authorized to file for protection of plant varieties. A "breeder" means a person, a group of person or farmer or a group of farmer's or any institution which has bred, evolved or developed any variety.

HOW TO APPLY?

The application involves filling up of and filing of Form 1 for a New variety, extant variety and farmer's variety, or a Form 2 for an Extant Variety, along with a Technical Questionnaire associated with the Forms. This must also be accompanied with a Denomination, an Affidavit that states that no terminator technology was used, complete passport data, a statement that gives details about the characteristics for novelty, distinctiveness, uniformity and stability, a Declaration that genetic material used for breeding of the variety has been lawfully acquired, and a disclosure of use of genetic material conserved by any tribal or rural families.

The application has to be filed at the following address: Registrar, Protection of Plant Variety & Farmers Right Authority, Govt. of India, Ministry of Agriculture, NASC Complex, DPS Marg, Opposite Todapur Village, New Delhi.

As of April 2008, the following crops are covered:

- Cereals: Rice, wheat, maize, sorghum, pearl millet
- Legumes: Chickpea, mungbean, urdbean, field pea, rajmash, lentil, pigeon pea
- Fibre crop: Cotton and jute.

TERM OF PROTECTION

The term of protection lasts for 20 years in U.S. from the date of filing the application, protects the inventor's right to exclude others from asexually reproducing, selling, or using the plant so reproduced. This protection is limited to one plant variety.

Under the Indian Protection of Plant Varieties & Farmers' Rights Act, protection for plant varieties lasts 18 years for trees and vines, while it is for 15 years for other crops.

7

Protection of Geographical Indications

K. SUBODH KUMAR
Head IPR – Confederation of Indian Industry &
APTDC, Hyderabad

Geographical indications are intellectual property rights. They contribute to sustainable development and fair trade because the production of GIs is rooted in particular regions and cannot be relocated. Therefore, GIs are important tools for all countries around the world, not only for economic and social reasons but also for upholding the intangible values in the knowledge pool of traditional practices for future generations.

This paper is an attempt to highlight the need for a coordinated action plan for GI protection and possible strategies to be formulated to leverage the Protected GI in national and International market. The case of GI Protection of "Pochampally Ikat" has been highlighted to provide a background for GI protection initiatives in India. The road ahead to leverage the protected the Protected GI and scope of work at the national and International arena is also summarized.

BASIS FOR GI PROTECTION

Geographical Indication[1] is one form of Intellectual Property in an Indication and:

- It originates from a definite geographical territory
- It is used to identify agricultural, natural or manufactured goods

[1] Classified as one form of Industrial Property. Examples of GI: Darjeeling tea, Roquefort Cheese, Tequilla etc.

- The manufactured goods should be produced or processed or prepared in that territory
- It should have a special quality or reputation or other characteristics.

The features of GIs, which in contrast to other IPRs make it relatively more amenable to the Indian customary practices particularly of our local indigenous communities. First, knowledge underlying the GI remains in the public domain. Second, in most jurisdictions, the rights can be held in perpetuity, in particular as long as the good-place-quality link is maintained. Finally, the scope of protection of GIs, such as the absence of a right to assign and its basis as a collective right, make it consistent with cultural and traditional rights.

INTERNATIONAL SCENARIO

There are various international agreements[2] which grant some kind of protection for GIs as intellectual property rights. Because of its availability and the number of signatory members, the WTO (World Trade Organization) TRIPs Agreement (an agreement on trade related intellectual property rights) of 1994 is currently the principal international instrument for protecting and defending GIs.

This agreement provides for two levels of protection: A basic protection fixed in Article 22 for all products which is determined by an act of misleading the public or unfair competition; and an additional protection fixed in Article 23 solely for wines and spirits which prevents any incorrect use of GIs on this type of product.

Convinced of the vulnerability of the GIs of our country in the international arena, India, along with a host of other like-minded countries (including the EU, Bulgaria, China, the Czech Republic, Hungary, Liechtenstein, Kenya, Mauritius, Nigeria, Pakistan, the Slovak Republic, Slovenia, Sri Lanka, Switzerland, Thailand and Turkey etc.) has been fighting at the WTO for quite some time now, for an extension of the ambit of Article 23 (henceforth 'extension') to cover products other than wines and spirits as well. According to them, producers of any good and not only those of wines or spirits have a legitimate interest in protecting their respective GIs from such exploitation. Hence, they demand that all the GIs, irrespective of the

---

[2]The Paris Convention for the Protection of Industrial Property (1976), The Madrid Agreement for the Repression of False or Deceptive Indications of Source (1981), Lisbon Agreement for the Protection of Appellations of Origin and Their International Registration (1958).

product category, should be afforded protection both under Article 22 and Article 23 of TRIPs, which are complementary to each other.

However, countries like the United States, Australia, New Zealand, Canada, Argentina, Chile, Guatemala, Uruguay etc., are strongly opposed to the 'extension'. This group argues that the existing (Article 22) level of protection is adequate, and that providing enhanced protection would be expensive. Furthermore, they perceive a better protection of GIs as a barrier to trade because, in their view, ensuring better protection of GIs would close markets or affect the producers' activities since certain products would have to be relabeled. For this reason, the debate has very often been described as one between the 'Old World' and the 'New World'.

NATIONAL SCENARIO

The GI Act in India was formulated as part of the exercise in the country to set in place national intellectual property laws in compliance with India's obligations under the TRIPs Agreement. Under this Act, which has come into force with effect from 15th September, 2003, the Central Government has established the 'Geographical Indications Registry' with all India jurisdictions at Chennai, where the right holders can register their respective GIs. After a GI is registered any person claiming to be the producer of the good designated by the registered GI can file an application for registration as an authorized user. The GI Act is administered by the Controller General of Patents, Designs and Trade Marks – who is the Registrar of Geographical Indications. Figure 1 shows a quick snapshot of the Indian Act related to Geographical Indications and the relevant sections associated with it.

Some of the important GIs filed in our country encompass textile, handicraft, agriculture and industrial sector. Darjeeling Tea was the first GI to be granted in India and Pochampally Ikat was the first GI to be granted in the Indian Traditional Sector. Mysore Silks, Aranmulla Metal Mirror, Chanderi Sarees & Orissa Ikat & Kulu Shawls are some of the granted GIs in India.

SYNOPSIS OF THE CASE FOR GI PROTECTION: POCHAMPALLY IKAT

The Genesis of the Idea

The idea to have an intellectual property protection to the Pochampally Ikat originated from the purpose of finding a solution to the age old problem of Pochampally weavers – large mills copying the Pochamapally Designs

An Act to provide for the registration and better protection of geographical indications relating to goods

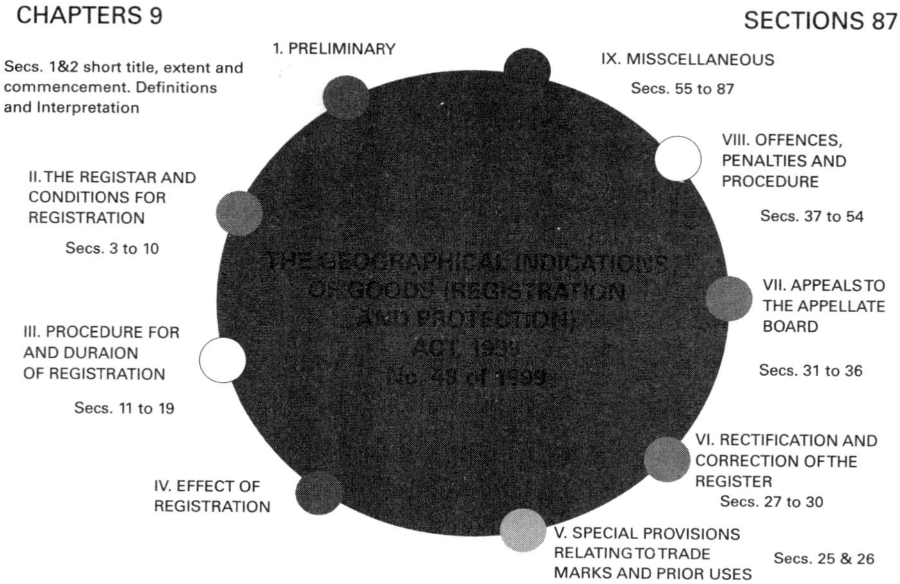

Figure 1. Snapshot of the Indian Act related to Geographical Indications and the relevant sections associated with it.

wherein they could produce the same design at a lower cost. The weavers approached Govt. of Andhra Pradesh for a possible solution.

The Objectives formulated

- Protecting the name "POCHAMPALLY IKAT"
- Preventing the unauthorized use of the name "POCHAMPALLY IKAT"
- Identifying and providing suitable Intellectual Property Rights protection i.e. thorough the Geographical Indication Act
- Promotion of POCHAMPALLY IKAT as a brand
- Creating IPR awareness amongst the weavers and the tangible benefits of Intellectual Property Rights Protection
- Policy formulation of identifying natures/types of violations and proposed action for IPR enforcement.

The Modus Operandi

- A team comprising members from Andhra Pradesh Technology Development & Promotion Centre (Promoted by CII, Govt. of AP & TIFAC),

Textile Committee, Govt. of India, Weavers Service Centre, Govt. of India, NABARD & Attorneys visited the Pochampally Site to ascertain the Uniqueness of Pochampally Ikat and whether it can be protected under the Geographical Indications of Goods & Services Act of 1999.

- A series of sensitization workshop was conducted for the benefit of the weavers to enable them to understand the tangible benefits and implications of Intellectual Property Protection.
- A careful documentation process was carried out to bring out the Statement of Case for filing the Geographical Indication application of Pochampally Ikat.
- The application was filed for Geographical Indications on 15th December, 2003. Subsequently, the expert committee from Govt. of India visited the Pochampally site on May 2004 to ascertain the facts. The expert committee was led by the Controller of Patents, and Designs & Trademarks, Govt. of India.
- The expert Committee brought out its recommendations and this was answered by the team mentioned above. The case of Pochampally Ikat was found meritorious by the Expert Committee.
- On December 31 2004, Pochampally Ikat was awarded the GI Registration.

What is guaranteed by GI Protection?

- It confers legal protection to the registered GI in India
- Prevents unauthorized use of goods associated with the registered GI by others
- Registration affords better legal protection to facilitate an action for infringement. The registered proprietor and authorized users can initiate infringement actions. The authorized users can exercise the exclusive right to use the geographical indication
- It promotes economic prosperity of producers of goods produced in a geographical territory.

CONCLUSION

- A number of limitations to the potential of GIs must be acknowledged. For instance, as the knowledge underlying a GI remains in the public domain, its misappropriation (qua biopiracy) is not protected against. As such, GIs should be considered a part of a wider set of policies measures that seek to protect and reward indigenous knowledge. This raises the possibility of complementary, though overlapping, IPRs covering similar subject matter. By way of example, consider handicrafts:

the technical content may be protected as a technical idea, while the cultural value as form of expression and its distinctive characteristics through marks or indications of geographical origin.

- GIs as club goods: organization and governance of supply chains, achieving coherence and authenticity between different firms and within each firm's supply chain raise substantial collective action problems. It should be recognized that as GI pre-exist their registration and protection, any reorganization of supply chains requires modifications to well-established commercial relations and distribution channels. Quasi-public institutions, representing the interest of all firms in the supply chain, are best placed at resolving these collective action problems.
- Some of the important steps to be taken on internationally for leveraging GIs across the world as a competitive tool:

  - A multilateral register for geographical indications (TRIPs): A simple, cost-effective system of world-wide registration for geographical indications so that farmers and SMEs can protect their GIs, even if they don't have deep pockets.
  - The extension of the additional GI protection (TRIPs): Ensuring that not only wines & spirits but also handicrafts, rices and teas can enjoy the benefit of not being copied by producers from other countries.
  - Ensuring market access for GI products: By asking WTO members, for a selected group of GIs, to remove prior trademarks and grant protection for GIs that were previously used or have become generic so that the GI products can gain market access.

8

Traditional Knowledge and Prospects of Protecting it Through Intellectual Property Legal Regime

R. SAHA
Former Adviser
Department of Science and Technology, Delhi

INTRODUCTION

The topic of protecting traditional knowledge (TK), especially knowledge related to herbs, herbal formulations, folklore, art and crafts through a legal framework has been a topic of debate and discussion globally and in particular in India for quite some time. More often than not the general prescription is that traditional knowledge possessed by societies should be protected under the legal framework of intellectual property rights (IPR). The true nature of IPR is not comprehended by those writing the above prescription and the relationship between TK and IPR is often lost sight of. The concern and a legitimate urge to protect TK is relatively a recent development triggered off perhaps by the Convention on Biological Diversity (CBD) which stipulated that each country has a sovereign right over the biological diversity possessed by it, and setting up of the World Trade Organization (WTO) which brought the IPR matters upfront as an essential instrument for international trade. Article 16 of CBD states "The contracting parties, recognising that patents and other intellectual property rights may have an influence on the implementation of this Convention, shall cooperate in this regard subject to national legislation and international law in order to ensure that such rights are supportive and do not run counter to these objectives." Similarly the WTO Preamble envisages expansion of the production and trade in things and services with optimal use of the world resources in accordance with the objectives of the sustainable development, seeking both to protect and preserve the environment. Therefore one can see a commonality in the thought process on the use of biological resources. Internationally, many forums especially, World Intellectual Property Organization (WIPO), have been engaged in debates on this topic for the last decade. Many study papers have been produced but no consensus has emerged so far among the member countries of WIPO.

SOME TRIGGERING FACTORS FOR THE DEBATE

It may be difficult to identify exact reasons for this debate in a chronological order. It was perhaps being felt in many developing countries that their bio-resources have led to discovery/invention of many new medicines. With a new global perspective emerging on the trade front the realization about the use of TK in designing new drugs, agrochemicals, cosmetic formulations and food recipes became widespread. It was also reported that companies had been active in collecting information about the use of plants and other biological materials (from developing nations) for getting new leads for deriving new products. Often the leads are obtained by talking to village seniors, local doctors etc., which actually bring in tremendous saving in time in screening new molecules. With the emergence of TRIPs which allows proprietorship of knowledge and its products, a new sense about the legitimacy of such proprietorship got developed. Holders of TK don't seem to get anything in return for sharing the knowledge (benefit sharing). Some recent developments regarding patenting of already known things such as wound healing property of turmeric and patenting of Ayahuasca plant have brought the issue in the forefront.

CASE OF TURMERIC PATENT

A US patent was granted to University of Mississipi, USA with Das, Cohly and Jackson as inventors claiming wound healing property of turmeric when applied locally or orally in 1995. This patent was first located by the author and brought to public knowledge. This caused adverse public reaction in India at all levels because the use of turmeric as wound healing agent is known to Indians for centuries and turmeric is used in many households in India for this purpose. The US Patent and Trademark Office was approached to re-examine the patent for its revocation by CSIR. As evidence, a Persian document of late 19th century highlighting the use of turmeric was produced before the USPTO which accepted the evidence and cancelled all the claims. This was considered a big step in attracting world attention to misappropriating TK through patents. The decision of USPTO was in line with the fact that any product or process or method cannot be patented if it is already known in public domain.

CASE OF AYAHUASCA PATENT

Baisteriopsis cappi plant is known to about 400 tribes in and around Amazon for centuries. Plant is used for making ceremonial drink "ayahuasca". The plant has religious and medicinal importance. A US patent was granted to a US citizen, Mr. Miller in 1986 for a new variety of the plant located/discovered by him in a domestic garden in a rain forest of South America. This plant was reproduced asexually from cuttings by Mr. Miller. The Coordinating Body of Indigenous Organizations of the Amazon Basin (COICA) knew about the patent in 1994. It was learnt that Mr. Miller intended setting up a pharmaceutical lab, in Ecuador to process ayahuasca plant and that the USA and Ecuador were planning a bilateral IP reciprocity agreement. COICA feared that indigenous people will lose their rights over their sacred plant. COICA approached USPTO for reexamination of the patent. USPTO rejected the claims on the grounds of novelty on November 5, 1999. Ecuador did not go ahead with the bilateral agreement in view of these facts. The case was reexamined by the USPTO and it reinstated the claim on April 17, 2001.

NATURE OF TRADITIONAL KNOWLEDGE

It is quite difficult and perhaps a complex exercise of logic to define traditional knowledge (TK). There could be many reasons which render the task very difficult and some of them are given below:

- TK is not limited to any specific field of knowledge.
- An element of long past is associated with TK. Origin of TK is often indeterminate. TK represents the entire field of human endeavour.
- It is an aggregation of many different fields of knowledge viz. science, technology, arts, music, dance, folklore, beliefs, ethics, medicine, biodiversity conservation, agriculture, environment and so on.
- Its development has not been systematic but has developed as a continuous response to environment, more as an experiential knowledge system.
- TK is usually held collectively and not by a single individual.
- Most TK is transmitted orally and little documentation exists for TK in many societies.

- TK systems are frameworks for continuing creativity and innovation and are deeply rooted in social and cultural systems.
- Any one is free to add to the knowledge system. It is extremely difficult to determine individual contributions and also community contributions in the TK as we see it today.
- Over the years geographical boundaries among nations have changed as new nations have emerged, large scale migration of population has taken place and massive diffusion of knowledge has taken place across communities, societies and nations. Ownership of TK is extremely difficult to determine individual contributions and also community contributions in the TK as we see it today.

POSITIONING OF TRADITIONAL KNOWLEDGE VIS-À-VIS OTHER FORMS OF IPRS

IPRs are linked to human creations which are globally novel at the time of putting a claim for proprietary of such creations and many a times it is linked to originality. Novelty comes into play when one is talking in terms of patents, designs and new plant varieties. Originality is predominantly associated with copyrights. The second important aspect of IPR is that most of the rights have fixed term of protection. In other words there is no legal protection after the expiry of the fixed term. However, it is possible to extend the term of trademarks and geographical indications to infinite time (theoretically) or for a very long time by payment of prescribed fees to the government. Further, the IPR are owned by legal entities or individuals or group of individuals. These rights cannot survive for the fixed term or even part of the fixed term unless the owner renews the rights from time to time as prescribed in the law by paying prescribed fees to the government. Renewal of copyrights is not prescribed in the law. TK when viewed from the above perspective does not meet the requirement of novelty as TK is publicly known for a long period of time. The prescribed terms of protection are very short to embrace TK. The issue of ownership of TK may be difficult to resolve as the origin of TK cannot be established in most cases. Secondly, communities are not really legal entities in true sense and they cannot own the TK.

Does it mean that nothing related to TK can be covered through the modern IPR system? The answer is no because the TK can be improved or modified or packaged in a different form. The modification or improvement or new form could be candidates for patents provided they meet the legal requirements. For example, if someone invents an injectible form of turmeric, then the new form can be a candidate for patent.

All IPR except trademark, geographical indications and trade secret have fixed term whereas TK relates to much longer period. Hence, there is a compatibility problem. The term of IPR is not suitable for TK.

Trade secret seems a possible route. However, its applicability in view of population migration from one place to another, inter-community marriages etc., cast a doubt on maintenance of secrecy.

Geographical indication and trademark, especially community trademark, would work in many cases. However, community trademark may not find any application in short term.

NATIONAL EFFORTS – INDIA'S INITIATIVES

A multi-pronged, multi-agency, multi-level, interdisciplinary, participatory and transparent approach has been taken by India to avoid misuse and misappropriation of TK, provide due benefits to the preservers of TK through benefit sharing and keep biological resources outside patents regime by creating new legal frameworks, databases and institutions. The Patent Act has been amended to have the following provisions.

Discovery of any living thing or non-living substance occurring in nature is not patentable. Plants and animals in whole or any part thereof are not subject matters of patents. An invention which, in effect, is traditional knowledge or which is aggregation or duplication of known component or components is not patentable. If an invention is anticipated having regard to the knowledge, oral or otherwise, available within any local or indigenous community in India or elsewhere is not patentable. Further, a patent document utilizing a biological material must disclose the source and geographical origin of biological material in the specification.

Protection of New Plant Variety and Farmers' Rights Act has provisions for protection of extant variety and new plant variety. In case an indigenous seed is used for producing a new variety there is a provision for sharing the benefits with the farmer(s) who provided the original seeds. Farmers have been given the rights to reuse seeds from their crops for the next crop. Similarly, the National Biodiversity Act stipulates that prior informed consent from National Biodiversity Authority should be taken for exploiting biodiversity of the country. In case R&D efforts based on the utilization of biological resources lead to generation of intellectual property rights and subsequent commercialization, benefits should be shared with the communities. The national legislation on protecting geographical indications is also a step in the direction of protecting TK. All the above legal frameworks tend to safeguard and preserve TK.

The government has set up National Innovation Foundation (NIF), Patent Facilitating Centre (PFC) and Traditional Knowledge Digital Library (TKDL) for looking at different aspects of TK. The NIF aims at developing sustainable technologies by scouting, spawning and sustaining grassroots innovations, diffusing grassroots innovations to a larger section of the society and translate these innovations into self supporting activities. The TKDL has been set up to digitize traditional knowledge. It has documented the ayurvedic formulations written in the ayurvedic textbooks in digital form. The database is being provided to various patent offices under an agreement. The database is available in many languages such as English, German etc. PFC is engaged in, among other things, keeping a vigil on patents being granted which may be related to the Indian TK.

HOW TO PROTECT PLANTS RELATED PATENTS UNDER THE TRADITIONAL KNOWLEDGE UMBRELLA

One of the common themes of patents associated with TK are the patents related to the use of plants in different applications. Some of the patentable subject matters would be combination of different plant materials, extracts and their combinations, process for extraction and process for preparing compositions. It would be useful to keep the following in mind while drafting a patent specification dealing with plants.

- Plants have to identified clearly.
- If the therapeutic value of plant part is different from the traditional use, the parts have to be labelled.
- If invention focuses on the percentage of different constituents (plants), percentages should be clearly disclosed and examples should be given.
- If a product cannot be defined on the basis of chemical composition, it can be defined through product by process method.
- It is good to characterize plant extracts. To differentiate from prior art, some fingerprints technique may be used.
- Dosage forms, dosage schedules should be given.
- Some kind of toxicity results should be given in case there is radical departure from traditional practices.
- An applicant should disclose the invention accurately and adequately. If the invention is a pharmaceutical, the applicant should provide the evidence that this invention has the claimed pharmacological effect. This may include providing *in vivo* (proven animal models) and *in vitro* test results.

- It would be better if test results are statistically significant.
- State taxonomical names of plants used. If taxonomical names are not available, common names may be given. Include as many names as possible to cover different regions.
- The principle of unity of invention must be kept in view while drafting claims.

CONCLUSION

Protection of traditional knowledge and products derived from that is a complex subject and therefore, it is necessary to develop a clear-cut understanding on IPR laws and their relationship with various aspects of TK. It may be emphasized that TK in its known and existing form is not a subject matter of protection under most forms of IPR. It certainly cannot be patented.

9

Trade Secrets

Trade secret is any information that is generally not known or reasonably ascertainable. The nature of information may be anything like formula, recipe, practice, process, design, instrument, factory layout, compilation of information, and so on. The reason for rendering such information as a secret is so that the owner can gain an economic advantage over competitors. Trade secrets is generally the name given by most intellectual property experts, however, information held as secret may also be referred to as "Confidential Information", or "Classified Information", or some such variation.

Among all the forms of intellectual property, trade secrets are unique in that the protection is offered to the information for NOT disclosing the contents. For every other form of intellectual property, the protection is offered for whatever is disclosed to the public. The protection offered by other forms of intellectual property is typically the right to prevent or exclude others from making, using, selling, importing, or offering for sale the disclosed information. In contrast to this, trade secrets do not offer this level of protection because of the secrecy involved. The protection can be extended only as a remedial action taken against those who have acquired the information through wrongful means. Further, the information under a trade secret can be held for an indefinite period of time, as opposed to the other forms of intellectual property, whose protection periods expire after a certain period of time.

One of the most famous examples of a trade secret is the formula for Coca-Cola drink. The company had chosen not to patent the formula, and this formula has been kept in trade secret shroud for over a hundred years quite successfully. Similarly, the recipe for Colonel Sanders fried chicken is also a trade secret. Recently, AMD and Intel have been involved in some lawsuits against their employees for having stolen valuable trade secrets involving their chip design.

LEGISLATIONS FOR TRADE SECRETS

Article 39 of the TRIPs agreement provides for the jurisdictions to provide for the appropriate protection of trade secrets as follows:

1. "... Members shall protect undisclosed information in accordance with paragraph 2 and data submitted to governments or governmental agencies in accordance with paragraph 3.
2. Natural and legal persons shall have the possibility of preventing information lawfully within their control from being disclosed to, acquired by, or used by others without their consent in a manner contrary to honest commercial practices so long as such information:

   (a) is secret in the sense that it is not, as a body or in the precise configuration and assembly of its components, generally known among or readily accessible to persons within the circles that normally deal with the kind of information in question;
   (b) has commercial value because it is secret; and
   (c) has been subject to reasonable steps under the circumstances, by the person lawfully in control of the information, to keep it secret.

3. Members, when requiring, as a condition of approving the marketing of pharmaceutical or of agricultural chemical products which utilize new chemical entities, the submission of undisclosed test or other data, the origination of which involves a considerable effort, shall protect such data against unfair commercial use. In addition, Members shall protect such data against disclosure, except where necessary to protect the public, or unless steps are taken to ensure that the data are protected against unfair commercial use."

However, no jurisdiction has enacted a set of laws specifically geared towards the protection of trade secrets. The closest any country has come to this is the Uniform Trade Secrets Act UTSA by the U.S. In this act, among other things, a definition of trade secret is provided, the manner of misappropriation or wrongful acquisition of trade secrets is given, and the remedies that can be expected by the affected party are also given. Other countries rely on other laws and act within the legal framework already available to establish the protection of trade secrets.

NATURE OF TRADE SECRETS

As trade secrets comprise information of a very delicate and sensitive nature, it makes sense for those responsible for its upkeep to maintain the secrecy over it. Indeed, TRIPs agreement states in Article 39 Paragraph 2(c) "that has been subject to reasonable steps under the circumstances, by the person lawfully in control of the information, to keep it secret." This implies that any information considered to be a trade secret must be appropriately marked and appropriate steps must be taken to ensure its protection. Otherwise, it may not be treated as a trade secret. Some simple examples would be to protect the information by keeping it in a safe, protecting the files using a password and revealing the password to only those who need to know, having a watermark or a header marking the contents to be of a confidential nature, and essentially ensuring such adequate precaution as is necessary.

WHO DO TRADE SECRETS PROTECT AGAINST?

The best way to protect a trade secret is not to reveal it at all. However, on several occasions, it may be necessary to reveal the trade secret to a select few individuals or groups. Employees or contractors working in or with an organization can be bound by iron-clad agreements that include strong confidentiality clauses. This may be on a routine basis such as an employee who has signed a confidentiality or a non-disclosure agreement during the time of employment, or by a contractor or a consultant, who can be made to sign a confidentiality agreement. While working with third parties, building a no-compete clause within any of the agreements is also useful. This clause essentially states that the third parties, while working with the organization, will not work with direct competition during the time of the engagement, and perhaps even for a period after the engagement is over. The extra time period after the termination of engagement is because trade secrets will still have value. Similarly, employees can also be made to sign an agreement that states that they will not work with direct competition immediately after the term of employment completes. This clause has to be scrutinized and carefully constructed to comply with any local laws, such as anti-competitive laws.

Protection can also be sought against those who obtained the trade secret through wrongful means, such as theft, industrial espionage etc. Further, anyone who is aware that the information being disclosed is a trade secret and still proceeds to acquire it may also be held responsible for misappropriation of trade secret.

Trade secrets, however, cannot be protected against reverse engineering and/or independent discovery. Both these forms of work are considered legitimate methods of acquiring information. This is a risk that trade secret owners should be aware of, and consequently, should be reasonably confident that either of these methods cannot lead to the exact information that is being protected.

HOW LONG DO TRADE SECRETS LAST?

Trade secrets last forever, or as long as it takes for one to stumble upon the information, or as long as it takes one to reverse engineer it. As mentioned earlier, the formula for Coca-Cola has lasted for longer than hundred years, and will probably remain a trade secret for a millennium, if necessary.

USING TRADE SECRETS

Trade secrets are generally used by organizations to keep the competition in the "dark" as to their plans towards latest product offerings, product components, method of producing etc. This will make the competition spend resources towards determining this information through legitimate means. Often times, even though the trade secret can be reverse engineered by a competition, the lead time provided by the trade secret is sufficient to gain market presence and establish a brand.

Some information that remains in the back end, such as customer ranking or pricing methods etc., may also be maintained as a trade secret. These may be information that is useful to build daily operations, and so, while competition can see and understand the daily operations, the reasoning may be lost to them without this valuable bit of information.

Another important kind of knowledge that may be kept under the trade secret banner is all the experiments that resulted in "negative" results. In a research environment, there may be several experiments that do not result in anything concrete, however, the knowledge gained through these experiments is always very useful, and helps to make choices in the future. This information can be kept as trade secrets, and hence, when the competitor attempts to reproduce the results or reverse engineer a product, at the very least they may have to go through the entire cycle of "learning" before arriving at the reverse engineered product.

ENFORCING MISAPPROPRIATION OF TRADE SECRETS

Whenever a trade secret owner becomes aware of someone else, such as a group of persons or an organization, in possession of the trade secret most likely obtained through wrongful means, then legal proceedings have to be initiated by the trade secret owner. Generally, to be successful in such cases, it will bode well for the trade secret owner to be able to prove in a court of law that the information:

- can indeed be classified as a trade secret, according to the guidelines given in Article 39 of TRIPs agreement, or any other prevailing law in that country, and
- came into the alleged culprit's hands through wrongful means.

The latter may be a difficult task, and very diligent investigations need to be undertaken to provide proof towards it.

Trade secrets provide a valuable and a powerful tool in the hands of a deft operator. They last forever, which in itself is a powerful incentive for someone to hold onto information as a secret. But, in today's global village environment, resources are available from every nook and corner of the world to be used in any endeavour. Given this, it is very difficult to hold trade secrets for any extended period of time. But in many circumstances, just enough lead time may be sufficient to make substantial gains in a market which may then lead to market dominance. This lead time may be provided by the appropriate use of trade secrets. Having information is not power in itself, but knowing how to use it is.

10

Introduction to Patents

The word "patent" derives from the Latin word *patere* which means "to lay open to public". Believe it or not one of the meanings of the word patent, as defined by Merriam-Webster Dictionary is "readily obvious or intelligible". Patents are typically granted to any new and useful process, machine, article of manufacture, or composition of matter in any technical field; and any new and useful improvements also. Patents thus facilitate disclosure of useful ideas to the public domain for the common good as it provides new and useful ideas. The exclusivity rights provided by patents can be suitably used for gainful exploitation by the inventor. This possibility of high remuneration also encourages creative intellectual endeavour in the public interest, thus spurring further innovations. The exclusivity rights may be exercised for only a fixed time period, following which new technology may be exploited by anyone. One important result of the patent system is that the availability of public record of inventions and patents thereof ensures that the knowledge is not lost to humanity.

Agreement on Trade Related aspects on Intellectual Property Rights, abbreviated as TRIPs is the underlying agreement which binds the signatories towards all matters related to intellectual property rights. This agreement is administered by World Trade Organization (WTO). The agreement lays down some minimum requirement in its articles, which the member countries are expected to adhere to. Over and beyond the minimum requirements, member countries may offer varying extensions in terms of rights, protection and so on. As stated earlier, the international arrangements related to intellectual property are co-ordinated by a United Nations organization – World Intellectual Property Organization (WIPO). Several countries, especially developing countries have relied on the technical support from WIPO for the implementation of the agreement and, indeed an entire IPR regime.

As mentioned, TRIPs agreement provides for broad outline of how the laws of each country need to be framed, and that all the signatory countries need to adhere to them. It must be stressed here that any intellectual property regime is jurisdiction or country specific, and each country has a slight variation towards implementing the laws and rules. However, there is an underlying common theme associated with these laws in various countries. The following sections describe some of the variations between the countries. These variations need to be understood to be able to suitably exploit the system so as to gain maximum protection from each jurisdiction.

CRITERIA FOR THE GRANT OF PATENTS

Article 27, paragraph 1 of TRIPs agreement states that "... patents shall be available for any inventions, whether products or processes, in all fields of technology, provided that they are new, involve an inventive step and are capable of industrial application. ... patents shall be available and patent rights enjoyable without discrimination as to the place of invention, the field of technology and whether products are imported or locally produced."

Any invention when presented to any patent office will be evaluated against four main criteria or Toll-Gates (TGs) to evaluate it:

TG 1: Belongs to any one of the Patentable Subject Matter; or contrarily, DOES NOT belong to any one of Non Patentable Subject Matter
TG 2: Is New or Novel
TG 3: Has an Inventive Step or is Non-Obvious
TG 4: Capable of Industrial Applicability or Useful.

The terms patentable subject matter, new, inventive step or industrially applicable are nowhere very clearly defined in the TRIPs itself and member countries are thus allowed the discretion to implement the agreement with their own unique interpretation. Each requirement will be discussed separately below.

In India, Section 2 of the Indian Patents Act, 1970 provides a list of Non-Patentable Subject Matter, while Section 13 lists the criteria of Novelty; in the USA, these requirements are governed by Title 35 of the United States Code (commonly referred to as 35 U.S.C.) § (the symbol representing Sections) 101-103 and in Europe, they are embodied in Article 52-57 of the European Patent Convention, 1973 (EPC), which is implemented in the member countries of EP by their domestic legislations.

I. Patentable Matter

As stated earlier, TRIPs agreement states that member countries may grant patents for any inventions, whether products or processes, in all fields of technology, provided that, they are new, involve an inventive step and are capable of industrial application. The agreement further states that member countries may exclude from patentability inventions that are contrary to *ordre public* or morality, including to protect human, animal or plant life or health or to avoid serious prejudice to life or health, to the environment; provided that such exclusion is not made merely because the exploitation is prohibited by their law.

We will now look at some important subject matter in light of patentability. In United States, patentability of organisms is not restricted. This is now a well accepted norm in U.S.A., and is based on a landmark summary judgment, for example, "fact that micro-organisms are alive is without legal significance for purposes of the patent law" (*See* Diamond v. Chakrabarty, 447 U.S. 303(1980)). Europe also allows for patenting of organisms as long as the experiments conducted and the ensuing patents result in a great benefit for mankind (EU Directive EC98/44). India allows patents for microorganisms only.

Theories, principles, mathematical equations, abstract ideas, laws of nature, and natural phenomena are not patentable subject matter. With regard to the latter two exceptions, they are excluded on the ground that they are already known and exist in nature; the inventor has actually not applied his skill and created anything new. With regard to the first exception, the essential logic is that ideas, thoughts and principles are fundamental truths and are common to all and exclusive to none. No person can preempt anyone else for using these ideas. Therefore the discovery of a new mineral or a new plant variety, mathematical formulas, laws of gravity etc., are not patentable. However, implementation of an idea that produces a concrete and tangible technical effect is generally considered patentable, i.e. the invention must be "a practical application" of the abstract idea, law of nature, or natural phenomenon. This is satisfied if either of the following situations occurs:

- the invention 'transforms' an article or physical object to a different state or thing; or
- the invention otherwise produces a useful, concrete and tangible result.

Patenting related to software and computer-related inventions have also led to many controversies. Currently, U.S. allows patents related to business methods utilizing computers and software (Summary judgment Diamond v. Diehr, 450 U.S. 175 (1981)). Europe and India have narrower scope than US for patents related to software. The Indian Patents Act, 1970 further states that "mere automation of a process by the introduction of software or a computer does not render a technology patentable, the software must be necessarily and inherently integrated with the system to make it patentable".

Generally, methods of treatment of human body and/or animals, such as surgical methods, are also not patentable in most jurisdictions. However, compositions, articles and instruments for use in the treatment are be patentable.

If any patent application bases the invention on a principle that violates the existing laws of nature, then it is deemed to contain non-patentable subject matter. Thus, a perpetual motion machine is not patentable. Further, almost all countries prohibit patents on atomic energy related technologies.

It is necessary to read a few sections of the law, or articles of the Act, together to understand whether a particular portion is applicable or not in a given situation. Thus, for example, to understand what is a patentable invention, one must first understand what is an invention, as per the definition in the given jurisdiction. Then, the subsequent sections of the law or the articles of the Act, must be interpreted in light of the original definition. Here, a few excerpts and the relevant sections are provided related to patentable subject matter.

In India, the definition of "Invention" as per the Indian Patents Act, 1970 is a new product or process involving an inventive step and capable of industrial application.

Indian patent laws do not provide a list of patentable subject matter, but instead, Section 3 of The Patents Act, 1970, India, and as amended in The Patents (Amendment) Act, 2005 provides a list of what **cannot** be patented, and are as follows:

(a) an invention which is frivolous or which claims anything obviously contrary to well established natural laws;
(b) an invention the primary or intended use or commercial exploitation of which could be contrary to public order or morality or which causes serious prejudice to human, animal or plant life or health or to the environment;
(c) the mere discovery of a scientific principle or the formulation of an abstract theory or discovery of any living thing or non-living substance occurring in nature;
(d) the mere discovery of a new form of a known substance which does not result in the enhancement of the known efficacy of that substance or the mere discovery of any new property or new use for a known substance or of the mere use of a known process, machine or apparatus unless such known process results in a new product or employs at least one new reactant. (This section has an explanation associated with it to give a better clarity towards some of the terms employed here.)

Explanation—For the purposes of this clause, salts, esters, ethers, polymorphs, metabolites, pure form, particle size, isomers, mixtures of isomers, complexes, combinations and other derivatives of known substance shall be considered to be the same substance, unless they differ significantly in properties with regard to efficacy. The mere discovery of any new property of new use for a known substance or of the mere use of a known process, machine or apparatus unless such known process results in a new product or employs at least one new reactant;

(e) a substance obtained by a mere admixture resulting only in the aggregation of the properties of the components thereof or a process for producing such substance;

However, an admixture resulting into synergistic properties of a mixture is not considered as mere admixture

(f) the mere arrangement or re-arrangement or duplication of known devices each functioning independently of one another in a known way;
(g) a method of agriculture or horticulture;
(h) any process for the medicinal, surgical, curative, prophylactic, diagnostic, therapeutic or other treatment of human beings or any process for a similar treatment of animals to render them free of disease or to increase their economic value or that of their products;
(i) plants and animals in whole or any part thereof other than microorganisms but including seeds, varieties and species and essentially biological proceses for production or propagation of plants and animals;
(j) a mathematical or business method or a computer program per se or algorithms;
(k) a literary, dramatic, musical or artistic work or any other aestheitc creation whatsoever including cinematographic works and television productions;
(l) a mere scheme or rule or method of performing mental act or method of playing game;
(m) a presentation of information;
(n) topography of integrated circuits;
(o) an invention which, in effect, is traditional knowledge or which is an aggregation or duplication of known properties of traditionally known component or components.

Further, Section 4 of The Patents Act, 1970, India states that "No patent shall be granted in respect of an invention relating to atomic energy falling within sub-section (1) of Section 20 of the Atomic Energy Act, 1962."

In the European situation, according to the European Patent Convention (commonly referred to by the abbreviation EPC), Article 52,

(1) European patents shall be granted for any inventions, in all fields of technology, provided that they are new, involve an inventive step and are susceptible of industrial application.

This definition of invention is very similar to the definition given in the TRIPs agreement.

(2) The following in particular shall not be regarded as inventions within the meaning of paragraph 1:

(a) discoveries, scientific theories and mathematical methods;
(b) aesthetic creations;
(c) schemes, rules and methods for performing mental acts, playing games or doing business, and programs for computers;
(d) presentations of information.

Article 53 of the EPC provides some exceptions to patentability:
European patents shall not be granted in respect of:

(a) inventions the commercial exploitation of which would be contrary to "ordre public" or morality; ...;
(b) plant or animal varieties or essentially biological processes for the production of plants or animals; this provision shall not apply to microbiological processes or the products thereof;
(c) methods for treatment of the human or animal body by surgery or therapy and diagnostic methods practised on the human or animal body; this provision shall not apply to products, in particular substances or compositions, for use in any of these methods.

As can be seen, these provisions are very similar to the provisions given in Indian Patents Act 1970.

Now looking at the U.S.A., 35 U.S.C. 101 defines Inventions patentable as:

> Whoever invents or discovers any new and useful process, machine, manufacture, or composition of matter, or any new and useful improvement thereof, may obtain a patent therefore, subject to the conditions and requirements of this title.

Based on this, courts in the U.S.A. have given a very liberal interpretation and the Supreme Court has gone on to hold that "*anything under the sun that is made by man*" is a statutory subject matter. The judiciary has, however, created certain exceptions to patentable subject-matter. A claim over abstract ideas, laws of nature and natural phenomena are held to be outside the four statutory categories of inventions.

THREE MAIN CRITERIA FOR PATENTABILITY

Once a determination has been made whether the invention as described or conceived does not fall under any one of the category of non-patentable subject matter as described, the next step is to determine if the invention qualifies for the grant of a patent. The three main criteria for doing so are:

- Novelty
- Non-Obviousness or Inventive Step, and
- Usefulness; or Industrial Applicability.

These concepts are discussed herein greater detail.

I. Novelty

Novelty in the context of an invention means that the invention not known before the earliest date of filing of the patent application. Any invention that is not new is not granted a patent because the object of patent law is to add new information to the public domain. Different types of novelty exist within this framework:

Relative Novelty is said to be present when a grace period exists from the date the invention was made known publicly before the earliest filing date. In some instances, U.S. and India follow this novelty, wherein, a one year period to file for a patent from the date the invention was made public exists.

Absolute Novelty is said to be present when any prior written or oral publication, demonstration or public use by anybody, anywhere in the world renders the invention as already known, and hence unpatentable. This form of novelty is used in Europe, and hence, generally, all forms of secrecy to protect an invention are followed until a patent application is filed with the appropriate patent office before making the invention public.

Local novelty is said to be present when only those publications, uses or sales that have taken place within that jurisdiction to be novelty destroying to the invention. Anything known, used, sold or published outside of the jurisdiction does not affect the patentability of the invention.

It should be mentioned here that, upon the filing of a patent application in one jurisdiction that is a member of the Paris Convention Treaty, a period of one year exists during which a priority can be claimed to the original filing, and a patent application can be filed in all the other member countries also within that one year period. Thus, as an illustration, if a patent application was filed in U.S. April 29, 2008, then, before April 28, 2009, patent application can be filed in other Paris Convention Treaty members such as EP, India, China, etc., and the application (refered as priority date in such cases) date will be considered the original filing date in U.S i.e., April 29, 2008. Thus, any act of publication, or sale or use in this interim period is not considered novelty destroying.

Section 13 of the Indian Patents Act, 1970 governs the novelty aspect of any invention, and it states:

> (1) The Examiner to whom an application for a patent is referred under section 12 shall make investigation for the purpose of ascertaining whether the invention so far as claimed in any claim of the complete specification ... has been anticipated by publication before the date of filing of the applicant's complete specification in any specification filed in pursuance of an application for a patent made in India ...;

Anticipation in this context means the reference cited is novelty destroying, i.e. it has disclosed the invention already. In order for an invention to be anticipated, a single prior art reference must expressly or inherently disclose the invention. The Section further states:

> is claimed in any claim of any other complete specification published on or after the date of filing of the applicant's complete specification, being a specification filed in pursuance of an application for a patent made in India and dated before or claiming the priority date earlier than that date.

For an explanation of the terms 'Claims' and 'Claimed', please see the Patents Contents Chapter 13 on page 99. For purposes of this chapter, it will suffice to understand that the invention is given in a particular portion of another patent granted in India.

> (2) The Examiner shall, in addition, make such investigation for the purpose of ascertaining whether the invention, so far as claimed in any claim of the complete specification, has been anticipated by publication in India or elsewhere in any document other than those mentioned in sub-section (1) before the date of filing of the applicant's complete specification.

Complete Specification as referred to in the Indian Patent System implies a patent application. The section 'Types of Patents' of this chapter gives an explanation about it.

Here, it is clear that an absolute novelty exists, and that is the case for the most part. There are situations wherein the relative novelty clause may be invoked, but the requirements are quite stringent.

U.S. law is governed by the statute 35 USC 102, which addresses novelty specifically.

35 U.S.C. 102. Conditions for patentability; novelty and loss of right to patent. This section consists of seven different parts, each of them dealing with different scenarios that may lead to novelty. The preamble for this section is as follows: "A person shall be entitled to a patent unless —". The preamble suggests that a patent application has been made or is intended to be made for an invention. The sections are numbered from (a) through (g) follow this preamble, each section joined to the other sections through the conjunction "or". Hence, if any one of the conditions is met, then patent will not be granted regardless of whether the other conditions are met or not.

Section (a) reads as follows:

(a) the invention was known or used by others in this country, or patented or described in a printed publication in this or a foreign country, before the invention thereof by the applicant for patent

This means that if the invention as described in the patent application is known or used in the U.S. (note the use of local novelty in this situation), then this will be grounds for rejection of the grant of a patent application. Similarly, if the invention as described in the patent application is patented or described in a printed publication in this or a foreign country (absolute novelty in effect in this situation) before the invention thereof, then a patent cannot be granted for the same.

Another important point to be noted here is that this section deals with the date of invention. In all jurisdictions, the date of the filing of a patent application is in essence, the date of the invention. However, U.S. gives a provision for proving the date of invention if it happens to be before the date of filing. There are some strings to proving the date of invention, which includes, among other things, a showing of diligent efforts towards working the invention.

(b) the invention was patented or described in a printed publication in this or a foreign country or in public use or on sale in this country, more than one year prior to the date of the application for patent in the United States

This section has a curious combination of various forms of novelty associated with it. First of all, it has a clause of "more than one year prior to the date of the application ..." which makes it a relative novelty being in effect. Further, it has a clause "... or in public use or on sale in this country ...", which makes it a local novelty. Thus the combination of these two clauses makes it a local relative novelty in effect for that clause. The other clause in effect i.e. "the invention was patented or described in a printed publication in this or a foreign country ..." coupled with "... more than one year prior to the date of the application ..." makes it a simple relative novelty.

(c) he has abandoned the invention

Abandoning of the patent application may happen through various means, which will be dealt with in later sections related to Prosecution.

(d) the invention was first patented or caused to be patented, or was the subject of an inventor's certificate, by the applicant or his legal representatives or assignee in a foreign country prior to the date of the application for patent in this country on an application for patent or inventor's certificate filed more than twelve months before the filing of the application in the United States, or

This clause states that a patent application that was originally filed outside of U.S. must be filed in U.S. within 12 months of the original filing, else one loses the right to do so.

(e) the invention was described in – (1) an application for patent, published under section 122(b), by another filed in the United States before the invention by the applicant for patent or (2) a patent granted on an application for patent by another filed in the United States before the invention by the applicant for patent, except that an international application filed under the treaty defined in section 351(a) shall have the effects for the purposes of this subsection of an application filed in the United States only if the international application designated the United States and was published under Article 21(2) of such treaty in the English language

This section is very crucial when handling situations wherein there are two patent applications by two different applicants for substantially the same invention, the first patent having been filed a little earlier than the second patent application. In some situations, the first patent application may not have been published when the second patent application was filed. This clause states that even though the first patent application was not published, and not known to public, it can be used to reject the second patent application.

(f) he did not himself invent the subject matter sought to be patented
(g) (1) during the course of an interference conducted under section 135 or section 291, another inventor involved therein establishes, to the extent permitted in section 104, that before such person's invention thereof the invention was made by such other inventor and not abandoned, suppressed, or concealed, or (2) before such person's invention thereof, the invention was made in this country by another inventor who had not abandoned, suppressed, or concealed it. In determining priority of invention under this subsection, there shall be considered not only the respective dates of conception and reduction to practice of the invention, but also the reasonable diligence of one who was first to conceive and last to reduce to practice, from a time prior to conception by the other

The last section talks about situations even if a person applies for a patent earlier, if a second person shows evidence of having made the invention earlier and did not abandon the invention, or purposefully suppress or conceal the invention, then this second person can ensure that the patent application made by the first person can be negated. It also goes on to state that there must be some level of diligence shown by the second person, else, the second person's may not be held valid.

Looking at the European view towards novelty, Article 54 of the European Patent Convention states that:

(1) An invention shall be considered to be new if it does not form part of the state of the art.
(2) The state of the art shall be held to comprise everything made available to the public by means of a written or oral description, by use, or in any other way, before the date of filing of the European patent application.

The first section gives a very simple definition for the term invention, with respect to novelty. The second section provides the definition to the qualifier for novelty, i.e. 'State of the Art'. 'Art' as used in this context means any technical field related to the patent application. Here it is fairly clear that the absolute novelty is in effect, and the interpretation of this article is fairly simple in that any invention must not be already known, in use, in a printed publication, or in any manner at all prior to the date of the invention.

(3) Additionally, the content of European patent applications as filed, the dates of filing of which are prior to the date referred to in paragraph 2 and which were published on or after that date, shall be considered as comprised in the state of the art.

The 3rd section handles situations that arise when a first patent application for a substantially similar invention was filed earlier with the European Patent Office, but was not available to public at the time of the filing of the second patent application, then the first patent application, despite its inherent secrecy, will be considered to be part of 'State of the Art'.

The article also does not give any leeway for having invented earlier but considers only the date of filing. Thus, for all practical purposes, the date of filing of the patent application with the patent office is the effective date of invention.

Some exceptions to the absolute novelty clause do exist in the statutory clauses of the European Patent Convention, however these are applicable only in very specific situations, such as "an evident abuse in relation to the applicant or his legal predecessor", or "the fact that the applicant or his legal predecessor has displayed the invention at an official, or officially recognised, international exhibition falling within the terms of the Convention on international exhibitions signed at Paris on 22 November, 1928 and last revised on 30 November, 1972", and so on.

II. Inventive Step or Non-Obviousness

If the invention disclosed in a patent application is an insubstantial variation, or an obvious variant of something that was already known at the time the patent application was filed, then the invention is considered to be obvious in light of prior art, and hence, not patentable. It is important to note that the invention is considered in light of what was already known at the time of the invention (which is, for all practical purposes, the date of filing). In Europe and India, there is a variation to this rule, and is usually referred to as "Inventive Step". Novelty is determined before inventive step because the creative contribution of the inventor can be assessed only by knowing the novel elements of the invention.

Invention is considered to be obvious or lacking an inventive step if it does not go beyond the normal progress of technology but merely follows plainly or logically from the prior art, i.e. something which does not involve the exercise of any skill or ability beyond that to be expected of the person skilled in the art. At a very basic level, 'prior art' refers to all the knowledge that is accumulated prior to the priority date of the invention. For this purpose a person skilled in the art is presumed to be an ordinary practitioner aware of what was general common knowledge in the relevant art at the relevant date.

According to the Indian Patents Act, 1970, "inventive step" means a feature of an invention that involves technical advance as compared to the existing knowledge or having economic significance or both and that makes the invention not obvious to a person skilled in the art.

In U.S, 35 U.S.C. 103 Conditions for patentability; non-obvious subject matter.

(a) A patent may not be obtained though the invention is not identically disclosed or described ... if the differences between the subject matter sought to be patented and the prior art are such that the subject matter as a whole would have been obvious at the time the invention was made to a person having ordinary skill in the art to which said subject matter pertains.

This is a simple restatement of what has already been described about non-obviousness.

(c) (1) Subject matter developed by another person ... shall not preclude patentability under this section where the subject matter and the claimed invention were, at the time the claimed invention was made, owned by the same person or subject to an obligation of assignment to the same person.

The Section (c) states that the obviousness clause can be raised only when a third party makes a very obvious variation or obvious addition to an existing invention. If the same applicant for a patent application makes an obvious variation or obvious addition to a patented invention, then the obviousness clause will not hold good. This clause is applicable as long as the date of filing of the two patent applicators are close enough.

Article 56 of the European Patent Convention deals with the Inventive step and states:

> An invention shall be considered as involving an inventive step if, having regard to the state of the art, it is not obvious to a person skilled in the art. If the state of the art also includes documents within the meaning of Article 54, paragraph 3 (the content of European patent applications as filed, the dates of filing of which are prior to the date referred to in paragraph 2 and which were published on or after that date), these documents shall NOT be considered in deciding whether there has been an inventive step.

The second sentence of the section states that any European patent application for a substantially similar invention was filed earlier with the

European Patent Office, but was not available to public at the time of the filing of the second patent application, then the first patent application will not be considered to determine the inventive step. As stated earlier, these documents will be considered only for determining 'State of the Art' and more relevant towards determining novelty.

III. Industrial Applicability

The final requirement for patentability is that it must be useful. This requirement has a very simple policy basis. It is based on the logic that resources of the state in terms of prosecution, registration etc., must not be wasted on something that is merely theoretical and academic. Unless, it can be put to some kind of use to achieve a result or a goal, it will not be granted. The grant of a monopoly is futile when the invention is of no utility. It is also a waste of resources for the inventor himself unless he can reap benefits / profits of the patent, which would happen only if the invention is producing a useful result.

Section 2 (1) (ac) of the Patents Act, 1970 states that '"Capable of Industrial application", in relation to an invention, means that the invention is capable of being made or used in an industry.'

Article 57 of the European Patent Convention states that 'An invention shall be considered as susceptible of industrial application if it can be made or used in any kind of industry, including agriculture.'

The laws in most jurisdictions are different from U.S. law which states that anything that is USEFUL is patentable, regardless of whether it is applicable in industrial situations or not. Here, 35 U.S.C. 101 is applicable, which does not provide for any narrowing down of the scope further from 'being useful'. For illustration of the difference between "useful" and "industrially applicable", the reader is directed to U.S. Patent #6,293,874 titled "User-operated amusement apparatus for kicking the user's buttocks". This is a patent which is perceived to be useful, but not industrially applicable. Hence, it may not be granted in jurisdictions like Europe or India.

UNITY OF INVENTION

There is a principle in all the patent laws which states that "One Patent Application for One Invention". In other words, a patent application can relate only to one invention or a group of closely related inventions. One invention is generally determined by the inventive concept that the patent application is dealing with. This provision ensures that several inventions are not unfairly covered under one patent application. Unity of invention also makes the classification of patent documents easier, which makes administration tasks easier.

PATENTS NOMENCLATURE

There are different types of patents based on the type of filing that was chosen. Patents may be "Original", which means that particular patent application was the first to be filed as a complete application in that series. Thus, effectively, the date of filing of that patent application is the date of invention.

In some jurisdictions, such as India and U.S., one can file a "Provisional" patent application. This is done usually to inform the patent office of the intent to file a complete patent application within one year of the date of filing the Provisional, by giving a text containing some key aspects of the invention. The Original patent application, when filed can claim priority to the Provisional in such instances, and thus the date of invention is the date of filing the Provisional. In such cases, the Original patent application is said "to claim priority from" the Provisional application, and the date of filing of the Provisional is generally referred to as "Priority Date". The Original patent application may also be sometimes referred to as "Non-Provisional" patent application in U.S., and in India, it is referred to as "Complete Specification".

In U.S., there is a possibility that one or more patent applications could also be "Continuation" of an earlier filed patent application. This means that the patent application resulted from ongoing work that had already given rise to an earlier patent application. The priority date for a Continuation patent application is considered to be the date of filing from the Original patent application from which the Continuation patent application claims priority from.

A "Divisional" patent application results from the splitting of one single filed patent application (may be done for various reasons, see Chapter 16 on page 123 Patent Prosecution for details). Irrespective of the number of Divisional patent applications that arise from one patent application, the priority date for all of them will be the date of filing of the original patent application.

In U.S., some parts of a newly filed patent application can take priority from an earlier filed patent application. Such patent applications are referred to as "Continuation-In-Part" (oftentimes referred to as CIP). The priority date for the continued part of a CIP will be the priority date of the Original patent application, while the newly added material in the CIP can claim priority from the date of filing of the CIP only.

In some jurisdictions like EP and India, some small and minor improvements over existing patented technologies may be filed under the category of "Patents of Additions" or "Improvement Patents". Such patents have a certain manner in which they are drafted, which will be dealt with in the Chapter 14 on page 106 Patent Draft.

LIFETERM OF A PATENT

All patents have an effective term of 20 years from the earliest filing date of the non-provisional patent application. U.S. patents may sometimes be extended by a certain period of time usually to compensate for any administrative delays, and the exact number of days by which the term is extended will be indicated in the front page. The exclusivity rights provided by a patent are only during this period, following which the technology protected in the patent is available for use by the public.

MAINTENANCE OF A PATENT

All patents require initial filing fees and possibly several fees following it until it gets granted (*See* Chapter 15 on page 113 Filing Patent Applications & Chapter 16 on page 123 Patent Prosecution). After the grant of a patent, it requires to be maintained by payment of maintenance fees periodically. Failure to pay maintenance fees within a certain time period will result in loss of exclusivity rights, and the availability of the technology for public. Table 1 gives the different timelines associated with the payment of filing fees in the three main jurisdictions considered herein.

Data on maintenance of patents may be obtained from the respective patent offices through their website or upon written request.

Table 1 Different timelines associated with the payment of filing fees in the three main jurisdictions considered herein

Maintenance Fees	US	EP	India
First Maintenance Fee Due[1]	4 years from Date of Filing	2 years from Date of Filing	2 years from Date of Filing
Subsequent Maintenance Fee	Every 4 Years	Annually	Annually

[1] Comes into effect only after the grant of patent. In cases of patent being granted after the 2-year-period, maintenance fees for the interim period will have to be paid along with the granting fees.

11

Ideas and Intellectual Property Rights

Ideas occur to every person, in all possible situations, at any given time. Who among us have not woken up in the middle of the night with a brilliant idea for something we had been pondering for a long time? A common statement that can be heard following an exclamation of a "brilliant" idea is usually "It ought to be patented". But are all great ideas patentable?

We have already seen all the various forms of intellectual property rights, and what each one of them encompasses. Thus, when one expresses an idea, can one automatically claim rights over this idea? The answer, in most cases, is a categorical NO. The reason is that just a mere expression of ideas has very little value to another person. The only form of intellectual property right that can be assumed and asserted, in some circumstances, over an expression of an idea is copyrights.

Copyright provides a set of automatic rights over an expression in a concrete and tangible medium. This means that mere verbal expression of a concept or a thought as such won't be sufficient to procure any rights. It must be fixed in some tangible medium that is capable of being reproduced at any later point. Thus, if one performs an impromptu skit illustrating a certain point in front of an audience, this performance *per se* is not copyrighted material. However, the recording of this performance on a camera, or a detailed description about the performance is the copyrighted material. This form of intellectual property rights is easily available to everyone who is capable of actions. Indeed, every human being on earth, including a new born child, has been responsible for many different copyrighted material, whether we are all aware of it or not.

Another form of intellectual property that may be secured by the recording of an expression on a tangible medium is Trademarks. This could be, say for example, a short catchy phrase about a product, a slogan about some services, could be some clever acronym, or quite simply a coined word that doesn't mean anything at all yet. A combination of words, colours, and shapes could also be used for this purpose. But as was already seen in Chapter 3 on page 17 Trademarks, anything related to a trademark must be associated with a product or a service.

Similarly, as noted earlier, any creations of the intellect merely for aesthetic or ergonomic reasons will fall under Industrial Designs or simply Designs. The reasons for making aesthetic improvements may be manifold, and may even include better movement of merchandise by attracting a consumers' attention. But the fact still remains that it is an aesthetic improvement and hence can only obtain Design protection.

Once again, as mentioned earlier, as in all other forms of intellectual property protection, to obtain good protection, it starts with a clear documentation and illustration of the actual creation. In the case of Designs, clear drawings, and explanations if necessary, of the shapes and sizes, and any ornamental features associated with the article would be very helpful.

When an idea is expressed, regardless of whether it is a technical one or a general idea, as mentioned earlier, it can garner only copyright protection. For an idea to be able to obtain patent protection, it must be an invention. An invention is a technical solution to a problem. Thus, even stating something very deep and profound and extremely useful as "convert the sound emanating from the traffic noise into electrical energy thus solving the energy crisis" will not be sufficient to obtain patent protection. There needs to be more details that may include many things such as, the basis for making such a statement (any theoretical background, equations and/or relationships between various forms of energy), the manner of conversion (how does one form of energy convert into another), the equipment to be used, the materials suitable for such uses (piezoelectric materials, perhaps), and so on and so forth.

An invention is considered to have a minimum of two distinct stages associated with it: 'conception' followed by 'reduction to practice'. Conception is generally when the idea is expressed as something that is useful. In our example, it is the mere mention of the harnessing of energy from an atom. Reduction to practice is said to occur when the idea is applied to a problem with all the associated details being provided and demonstrated as being actually useful, based on theoretical principles of the subject in question. The reduction to practice may be 'constructive' reduction to practice or 'actual' reduction to practice. Constructive reduction to practice is said to occur when the demonstration is done on paper, by simulations, or by obtaining data that is suggestive of workability of the idea. Actual reduction to practice is when an actual prototype is built and demonstration of an actual product is done. Thus, ideas when generated must also be weighed as to its completeness, whether there is both conception and reduction to practice.

Besides the minimum requirements for patents (which you may recall should pass the 4 toll gates of patentable subject matter, novelty, non-obviousness or inventive step and utility or industrial applicability), an idea generated by anyone must also be considered for its strength as to whether it is patentable or not. In India, Section 3(f) explicitly states that "the mere arrangement re-arrangement or duplication of known devices each functioning independently of one another in a known way" falls under the category of non-patentable subject matter. Other jurisdictions may not explicitly anything like this, but it is now well understood that such ideas cannot obtain patent protection, despite the fact that this new idea may appear to be novel, non-obvious and useful. Let us consider an example here. It is known that a form of graphite is capable of leaving marks on smooth surfaces such as paper. It is also known that the latex when heated with sulphur for a sufficient time and, molded into a shape is capable of erasing the mark left behind by the graphite-based marker, regardless of the surface. Now, if one ingeniously comes up with the idea to put together this 'graphite marker' and the 'eraser' together in one article, is this idea a patentable one? The answer, in short is NO! There is a statute in regulatory publications of almost every jurisdiction which provides that "a combination of two known things, despite seemingly a manufacture, is not patentable'. Indeed, the "invention" as mentioned here was patented back in mid-1800s in U.S. and a court decision invalidated the granted patent based on this doctrine.

Another hotly contested and sometimes quite confusing topic is the interpretation of the word "technical". The statement 'An invention must be a technical solution' seems an innocuous and seemingly simple, and a clear statement. But not in the hands of skilful lawyers!

Let us consider another idea here to illustrate this concept. A person who belongs to a predominantly rice-and-vegetables-eating culture travels to a far-off lands and cultures and notices that the other culture is a bread-and-meat-eating culture. On return, this person comes up with the idea of putting vegetables in between two slices of bread and consumes it. The select few who were invited to observe the enactment of this bright new idea are immediately in love with this idea. So, is this a patentable invention?

In this latter example, it must be noted that the concept of bread and vegetables and the individual consumption of each is known. So, it is a mere combination of two known things, so it wouldn't have taken much for "one skilled in the art" to come up with this idea. The other thing to be considered is that there is no particular improvement over the existing "art" or a problem addressed by this new idea. In other words, what was the problem with rice and vegetables being consumed the way it has been done for so many generations? One of the important facets of patentable ideas to be stressed is that there has to be a problem that is being solved. Alternately, the new idea provided must also be in a position to alleviate existing situations in some manner. This is conveniently defined in most jurisdictions as "technical effect". An invention must produce a concrete and tangible result that can be measured or estimated. One simple way to provide a technical effect in case of bread-and-vegetables example may be to pose the problem as: "Does it decrease the time taken to complete a meal?" or "Is the nutrition levels different in this meal?" etc. Thus, immediately, the study conducted and the data provided towards the invention would be very different than what would have been otherwise.

The following sections provide some details as to how some organizations have some standardized procedures to enable the identification and the conversion of ideas into patents as rapidly as possible.

CAPTURING IDEAS IN A STANDARDIZED FORMAT

Most organizations have a document with pre-prepared questions to capture any new idea to identify its patentability. Some of the questions posed there would include:

What is the problem solved?
What was done earlier to address this problem?
What is the idea mentioned here?
What is the new feature in this idea over what is already known?
How is this idea used in a typical situation? Explain the working of this idea in as much detail as possible.
Is there any data to demonstrate the usefulness of the idea?
Where else would this idea be useful?
Was a prototype built?

Having detailed answers to all of the questions given helps a patent practitioner to understand the idea, the patentability of the idea, and to find out if it truly is an invention.

TO PATENT OR NOT TO PATENT—WORTH PATENTING?

It is now obvious that an idea that is brilliant may not actually be patentable unless some criteria are sufficiently satisfied. In some instances, the utility of an idea that will make it patentable may be inherent, and requires some amount of reading background material on the topic. Especially in such instances, the utility of the idea will be ridiculously obvious to the person presenting the idea that the one asking the utility (albeit innocently) will be viewed with disdain. To illustrate this point from personal experience, a friend who exclaimed with great joy that he managed to fit a fan inside a computer casing close to the motherboard successfully, and that he was looking for patent protection was given a blank look and shrug off my shoulders, when he expected me to jump with glee with him. Only when he explained to me that heating was a huge problem in computers, and is subject of intense research activity in major corporations, that it occurred to me that his idea was definitely an invention and moreover, was a potential goldmine.

Several situations arise during the course of an idea discussion to convert it into a patent. From the patent application point of view, a judgment as to whether the idea is patentable or not is fairly easy to make based on the doctrines involved and the extent of the development of an idea. From a commercialization point of view, on the other hand, some other factors need to be taken into account. Getting patents granted is a fairly expensive process. Costs are incurred at various stages including invention discussion, drafting, filing, prosecution, translation, maintenance etc. Thus, obtaining maximum benefit from patents is vital for the sustenance of any organization. Benefits from patents may be realized through various means, such as licensing, infringement suits, selling etc. (*See* Chapter 19 on 167 IP Strategy).

Some of the key factors that need to be taken into account while assessing the worthiness of a patent include market data, existing products, extent of improvement, extent of exclusivity and identifiability. A patent when granted that results in a product has to be in a position to displace existing products at least to a certain extent so that the usefulness of the patent is reflected by the revenues generated from it. At the same time, potential infringers must be easily identified without a doubt as having infringed on one's patent thus swift action can be brought against the infringers. A patent having no identifiability built into it will be difficult to enforce, as there will always be doubt as to whether someone else is infringing on one's patents or not.

INVENTOR INTERVIEW

Inventor Interview is the formal process during which a patent practitioner, along with the attorney talks to the inventors involved in an invention, to get a complete picture of the invention provided. During this discussion, the technical field is talked about in detail, which sets up the background of the invention. This sums up basically what the state-of-the-art is, and what are the inherent problems in the field. Then, the idea itself is talked about in light of the background. Any data and references related to this are preferably made available to the practitioner ahead of time. The various aspects of the idea, and consequently the invention are discussed in as much detail as possible. All possible variations are to be churned out, and varying scopes of the invention are also given attention. (*See* Scopes of Inventions under Chapter 14 on 101 Patent Draft.) Before the end, discussing a rough draft of claims is also quite useful. (*See* Claims under Chapter 14 on 101 Patent Draft).

As we have seen now, an idea in itself is worth only as much as the words used to describe them. But once a certain level of detail is worked into these ideas, they become extremely valuable. Often times, the details will also assist in understanding the finer nuances of the concepts. This is the difference between outlines and actual stories for a movie. The outlines are very important in conveying a snapshot of what is contained within, but it cannot replace the actual story. Otherwise, no one will ever read 'Romeo and Juliet', but instead remember it only as love between a young couple that resulted in a great tragedy.

12

Public Disclosure, Bar Dates and Invention Record

PUBLIC DISCLOSURE

One of the basic conditions as set down by any law towards the procurement of any form of intellectual property is that of novelty and/or originality, i.e. it should not be already known, made, used, sold, or described in a publication. For instance, we have already seen that for an invention to be capable of procuring a patent, the criteria of novelty must be satisfied. Similarly, to obtain a Design registration, the criteria of new or original must be met. Such criteria are available for all the forms of intellectual property. (The exceptions to this are the Copyrights and Trademarks. In these cases, rights can be asserted even after making the creation available to public.) As it can be seen, it is very important that any new intellectual property should not be made available to the public until the appropriate procedures are followed to register the form of intellectual property before disclosing to the public. Further, registering any form of intellectual property is a form of disclosing to the public, along with other details such as the owner of the aforementioned intellectual property and the date of the actual conception, etc.

Let us consider the situation of an inventor coming up with an invention. As already mentioned (several times over), if an invention is already known, made, used, sold, or described, then it is not novel, because the invention is considered disclosed to the public. Let us consider this statement in greater detail, because it is important to understand the concept of novelty for obtaining the proper rights over any form of intellectual property. Generally, if the public at large already knows about an invention, or the knowledge concerning the invention is available to the public through the sale of products, for example, then public disclosure is said to have occurred. The effect of public disclosure is that the procurement of any type of intellectual property rights is severely compromised.

The first point to be noted concerns the word 'public'. Who constitutes 'public'? Anyone who is not an inventor or one of the inventors is considered to be part of the public. Thus, it is important to keep the public at large unaware of an invention until it is appropriately registered.

The next point to be taken into consideration is the word 'disclosure'. Any act by which the public becomes aware of the invention constitutes an act of disclosure. This could be through the sale of a product that contains the invention. As an example, if the invention is a method of processing signals, and the product sold in the market uses this method, then it is possible for the public to become aware of the invention by buying this product, and carefully studying it.

Another point to be noted here is the manner in which the information regarding the invention is made available to the public. It doesn't matter whether the information is available for free or whether one has to pay a premium price for it. The fact remains that any member of the public is privy to the knowledge.

Also, none of the laws in any jurisdiction discusses about who makes this disclosure. Thus, it doesn't matter if the inventors themselves made the invention known to the public, or whether someone else made that disclosure. Once again, the fact remains that the information is made available to the public, and hence the inventors' ability to procure the exclusively rights are severely compromised.

However, as was already noted, in jurisdictions which allows for the grace period by making use of the 'relative novelty', one's ability to procure the protection may still be available. But it is still hampered in other jurisdictions. So, it is very important to ensure the secrecy of any new creations until the date of filing the appropriate registration papers to procure the intellectual property rights. Subsequently, any amount of public disclosure CANNOT in any way hinder the procurement of the intellectual property rights for whatever that has been already filed for, as anything that is novelty destroying has to be before the date of filing.

So why would anyone disclose ideas and experimental results to the public at all? One reason could be that displaying a product containing an invention at a trade show or a conference will give the company some excellent visibility. This visibility will assist the marketing team to sell products. But such displays are considered to be public disclosure of the invention. The best way to mitigate this risk is by filing a patent application ahead of time.

In some cases, the invention may involve something which has to be in the public eye. This may be the situation in case of an invention involving an aircraft or a locomotive. Testing of the invention can rarely be achieved in a private situation. In such situations, almost every patent office will allow for exceptions wherein the testing or working has to be conducted in public.

If public disclosure severely compromises any commercializing activities, then this begs the question: Why would anyone disclose an invention to the public? The answer to that question lies in a further interpretation of the word 'public'. Anyone who is NOT bound by any legal authority, such as a contract, is considered to be public. This will raise a further question as to 'Why involve anyone else in my invention?' Any number of reasons exists for the involvement of others in an invention. This may include the use of laboratory equipment that is available in only one lab. Sometimes, the expertise in interpreting the results from an experiment may need to be taken from outside sources. In many instances, non-partisan objective results may need to be obtained from third-party laboratories for regulatory purposes. Off late, outsourcing work to third parties offshore is becoming quite fashionable for economic reasons. Also, for the preparation of the papers for filing with the appropriate authorities in the appropriate jurisdictions, the assistance of intellectual property agents and/or attorneys such as patent agents may be necessary, to whom details about the invention need to be disclosed.

To ensure that the invention does not become publicly known unless the inventors are ready to do so, air-tight agreements need to be signed by both parties.

AGREEMENTS

All the situations discussed earlier necessarily require the involvement of a third party. Ideally, before getting involved with third parties, air-tight agreements need to be in place. Several kinds of agreements can be invoked for a variety of different situations.

One of the most important types of agreement is the Non-Disclosure Agreement (NDA) or Confidentiality of Disclosure Agreement (CDA), or Confidentiality Agreement. Such an agreement typically contains clauses which cover the parties involved in the agreement, the nature of information that will be exchanged, the manner in which the exchange will take place, the confidentiality to be maintained, the extent and manner in which the information exchanged needs to be secured, the duration of the maintenance of the secrecy of information.

Other types of agreements can then be built over the signed NDA. Alternately, if the nature of the partnership between the involved parties are already well-known, then another agreement, such as a Joint Development Agreement (JDA), can be invoked without a separate NDA, which will include a Confidentiality clause within it. Similarly, patent agents' services may be employed by the execution of a suitable Consultancy Agreement. Typically, the other types of agreements will cover the nature of responsibilities of the involved parties, the extent of information that will be exchanged between them, the work products expected from them, etc. Any other terms and conditions, such as sharing of intellectual property resulting from the joint work should also be explicitly stated.

BAR DATES

As mentioned, there may be situations wherein on a particular date, an invention may become publicly known. This may be through a publication of a peer-reviewed article, the proceedings of a conference, a trade show, or some such occurrence. In other cases, a third party may be involved in the development of a project, possibly without a proper agreement in place. The date on which such an event has occurred is referred to as a 'Bar Date'. This is a momentous date in the course of a conception of any new creation, in that there is every possibility that you have lost the opportunity to procure suitable protection for your creation after this date. Thus, it is advantageous to anticipate this date and accordingly process the paperwork for procuring the rights prior to this date.

Further, involvement of any third parties in any part of the work, and the terms and conditions of the agreement, if any, and the expiration of the agreement must also be taken into account. The expiration dates may necessitate the urgent filing of papers before the date for various reasons (although, it is not uncommon to build in buffer dates after the termination of the agreement, such as a clause which states that, e.g. "the information shall be kept secret for two years after the termination of the agreement").

Any plans for a poster or an oral presentation in a conference must be taken into account, for as stated earlier, this may become novelty destroying. Jurisdictions utilizing the relative novelty gives a buffer time before filing the patent application, but only in that jurisdiction. It must be noted that such early public disclosure may result in inability to claim priority to the original patent application. (*See* Chapter 15 on 113 Filing Patent Application for details on filing in other jurisdictions by claiming priority).

RECORD OF INTELLECTUAL CREATION

Earlier, we have seen how ideas can strike us at any moment, at any situation. In such cases, there is a tendency to commit that idea to memory, and to repeat it to the relevant audience later. Alternately, the idea will be noted on the first surface that is conducive for recording it, such as a scrap piece of paper on the night stand, a paper napkin at the bar, etc. While such records are sufficient to explain the ideas, it is not necessarily the best method of providing any intellectual creation to other professionals or as courtroom evidence.

A record of intellectual creation is necessary for a variety of reasons, not least of which is to provide tangible evidence in court. A typical record is maintained in a single location like a single notebook. Any new idea ought to be typically recorded on the notebook, along with the date, and the name of the person(s) concerned with it. The events leading up to the conception of the idea may also be recorded, e.g. during the presentation given by someone; or at a meeting with team members. It is important to note the date of conception. The idea should be complete in its description, in that the notebook page should provide what the idea is, where it is useful, why the creator thinks it would work, and how it functions. Subsequently, experiments, if any, conducted and data obtained that supports the idea also needs to be recorded. The page numbers on which the experiments are continued from and to are recorded on the appropriate pages, so that another person reading the experiments can follow the thread of the idea quite easily. Finally, it is a good idea to have someone who is capable of understanding the experiments and the results has to witness it with the date on all the pages. This person CANNOT be part of the team, but should be an impartial witness.

During notebook updation, there should be no erasures, only strike-throughs to correct any written mistakes. Extraneous printouts such as spectrographic data, simulation data etc. need to be pasted on, and a closely related page must provide conditions under which the data was obtained, and a reference to the page on which the experiment was conducted.

Once a page has been read, understood and witnessed, nothing should be changed on that page. No more additions or deletions or changes are to be done. Any oversight that was caught at a later stage must be done at a later page with reference to the original page, although such practices are to be avoided at all costs for various reasons, least of which would be the credibility of the practitioner.

The maintenance of a notebook is very important in establishing the original creator of the intellectual property, such as to establish inventorship. Inventors are all those who contributed to the idea and made reduction to practice possible. Ultimately, inventorship will be determined by the drafted set of claims. (*See* Chapter 14 on 101 Patent Drafts). But ascertaining whether one is an inventor or not can be made facile by the production of clear written records delineating when, how, under what circumstances the idea was conceived and subsequently put to use, and who were all involved in it.

It must be noted that those who conduct experiments, obtain data and results, validate experiments are not inventors. Only those who contribute intellectually to the invention are inventors. Once again, it cannot be emphasized enough that maintaining diligent records of the circumstances under which the invention was made will establish this very clearly.

13

Contents of a Patent

Patent Contents can be generally classified into three broad sections: front-page, specifications, and claims.

FRONT PAGE

The front page of the patent contains a lot of useful information that is vital especially during search and analysis (*See* Chapter 17 on page 131 Search & Analyses of Patent Literature). Some of the important parts of the front page include:

Patent number: The presence of this number indicates that this is a granted patent and thus enforceable. It should also be noted that a granted patent also serves as prior art. Patent numbers are integers that are granted in a serial manner by the appropriate patent office.

Publication number: This number is important and provides the unique identification number with which the invention first came to public attention thus making it prior art. Typically a patent application is published 18 months after the date of the original non-provisional application. In US, the publication number can be split into three parts. The first two alphabets is "US" which represents the country of publication. Then the first four digits following it is the "year" of publication (in the yyyy format) which is then succeeded by an "integer" having several digits.

Here, a word about PCT publications is relevant. PCT applications, as we will see later in greater detail, are patent applications filed with the international organization, World Intellectual Property Organization (WIPO), and are then searched and examined on the 4 toll gates and are published. PCT publications follow similar numbering system, except that PCT publications are preceded by the alphabets WO. Typical PCT publication occurs 18 months from the original priority date.

In India, each patent application publication is identified by a serial number followed by a "/", then a three-alphabetical code to indicate the patent office in which it was filed, then another "/" and finally the year in the yyyy format. The four patent offices are represented by the following codes: CHE for Chennai, DEL for Delhi, MUM for Mumbai and KOL for Kolkata. It must be noted that these codes were different and more representative of the earlier names of the cities prior to their renaming.

Kind Codes: Patent and publication number further comprise a kind code associated with them that is appended to the end of the number. These two digit alphanumeric codes provide a brief snapshot of the history of the patent application with the patent office. The Tables 2–5 list the kind codes and their meaning in different jurisdictions.

Other useful information obtained from the front page include:

The names of *Inventors*

The name of the *Assignee* who owns the invention. In some jurisdictions, this is also represented as *Applicant.* It should be noted that the

Table 2 U.S. Patent Kind Codes

Kind Codes	Kind of Document
A1	Patent Application Publication
A2	Patent Application Publication (Republication)
A9	Patent Application Publication (Corrected Publication)
B1	Patent
B2	Patent
C1, C2, C3...	Reexamination Certificate
E	Reissue Patent
H	Statutory Invention Registration (SIR)
P1	Plant Patent Application Publication
P2	Plant Patent
P3	Plant Patent
P4	Plant Patent Application Publication (Republication)
P9	Plant Patent Application Publication (Corrected Publication)
S	Design Patent

Table 3 Indian Patent Kind Codes

Kind Codes	Kind of Document
A	Patent Application
A1	Granted Patent Specification

Table 4 European Patent (EP) Kind Codes

Kind Codes	Kind of Document
A1	Publ. of Application with search report
A2	Publ. of Application without search report
A3	Publ. of search report
A4	Supplementary search report
A8	Corrected title page of an EP-A Document
A9	Complete reprint of an EP-A Document
B1	Patent
B2	Patent after modification
B8	Corrected front page of an EP-B Document
B9	Complete reprint of an EP-B Document

Table 5 PCT Application Publication Kind Codes

Kind Codes	Kind of Document
A1	Publ. of the Int. Appl. with Int. search report
A2	Publ. of the Int. Appl. without Int. search REP.
A3	Subsequent Publ. of the Int. search report
B1	Publ. of amended claims
B8	Second modification of the First page
B9	Correction of a Complete Corrected Document
C1	Modified First page
C2	Complete Corrected Document

name of the Applicant or Assignee is as of the date of the application. Any subsequent changes to ownership may not be reflected on the patent application. Information related to change of ownership and/or licensee(s) of a patent applications or granted patent may be obtained from the patent office.

Title of the invention

Abstract of the invention which gives a brief overview of the invention disclosed in the patent application

Dates: For any granted patent, 4 different kinds of dates can be identified. These include the date of grant, the date of publication, the date of filing and the priority date. In the absence of any other priority filing, such as foreign filing or a provisional application filing, the date of filing is the priority date. Patent application publication, obviously, will not have any date of grant.

Classification codes are alphanumeric codes that indicate the technical field to which the invention is focused. Different patent offices have different ways of classifying, although there have been efforts into integrating the classification system into one international system recently. Concordant lists between different classification systems are also provided in some instances.

For IPC classification system used for PCT applications, please see the following link: http://www.wipo.int/classifications/fulltext/new_ipc/ipcen.html. The highest level of classification is given in Table 6.

US patent classification system comprises only numeric classes. For further details, please see the following link: http://www.uspto.gov/web/patents/classification/selectnumwithtitle.htm

For ECLA classification system that is used by EP, please see the following link: http://v3.espacenet.com/eclasrch?ECLA=/espacenet/ecla/index/index.htm. ECLA Codes are built on top of the IPC Classification Codes, with one extra level of classification beyond that of IPC Classification.

Several countries, including India, use the IPC Classification System directly for the classification of the patent applications filed in their respective patent offices.

The front page further comprises a Drawing that is most representative of invention as deemed by the inventors.

The front page of a granted US patent also gives a list of Citations that were considered by the examiner as being material to the patentability of the claims.

In PCT publications, a separate section called search report is also present, wherein all references considered material to patentability of the claims is given. These references are classified into the following categories, whose meaning is given in Table 7:

EPO Patent Publications share similar traits to that of a PCT publication.

Some US patents may have their lifetime adjusted for various reasons, which is reflected in the front page.

Table 6 IPC Classification Codes, Version 2008.04

Section	Subject
A	Human Necessities
B	Performing Operations; Transporting
C	Chemistry; Metallurgy
D	Textiles; Paper
E	Fixed Constructions
F	Mechanical Engineering; Lighting; Heating; Weapons; Blasting
G	Physics
H	Electricity

Table 7 Categorization Codes of references in a search report and their respective meanings

Category	Meaning
A	Document defining the general state of the art which is not considered to be of particular relevance
E	Earlier document published on/after the international filing date
L	Document which may throw doubts on priority claims or which is cited to establish the publication date of another citation or rather special reason (as specified)
O	Document referring to an oral disclosure, use, exhibition, or other means
P	Document published prior to the international filing date but later than the priority date claimed
T	Later document published after the international filing date or priority date and not in conflict with the application but cited to understand the principle or theory underlying the invention
X	Document of particular relevance; the claimed invention cannot be considered novel or cannot be considered to involve an inventive step when the document is taken along
Y	Document of particular relevance; the claimed invention cannot be considered to involve an inventive step when the document is combined with one or more other such documents, such combination being obvious to person skilled in the art
&	Document member of the same patent family

All the information provided in the front page of patents, regardless of the jurisdiction it is from, is preceded by a numeric code called INID codes, typically two digits, within parentheses. INID is an acronym that stands for "Internationally agreed upon Numbers for Identification of (bibliographic) Data". INID codes facilitate identification of the nature of the information even if the information is provided in a different language. For example the 75 represents "Inventors", and 54 represents "Title". A table showing some representative INID codes for some of the information is given in Table 8. Figure 2 gives a typical front page which contains all the relevant information, and the corresponding INID codes associated with the information. In this example, a PCT application is taken, and hence, there won't be a patent number associated with it.

SPECIFICATION

Patent document comprises several sections, some of whose titles include "Technical field", "Background", "Summary of the Invention", "Detailed

Table 8 Some representative INID codes and their meaning

INID Code	Explanation
10	Publication Number
12	Publication Authority
19	Filing Office
21	Application Number
22	Filing Date
25	Filing Language
26	Publication Language
30	Priority Data
43	Publication Date
51	Classification Code
54	Title
57	Abstract
71	Applicant/Assignee
72	Inventors
74	Agent
81	Designated States
84	Designated States

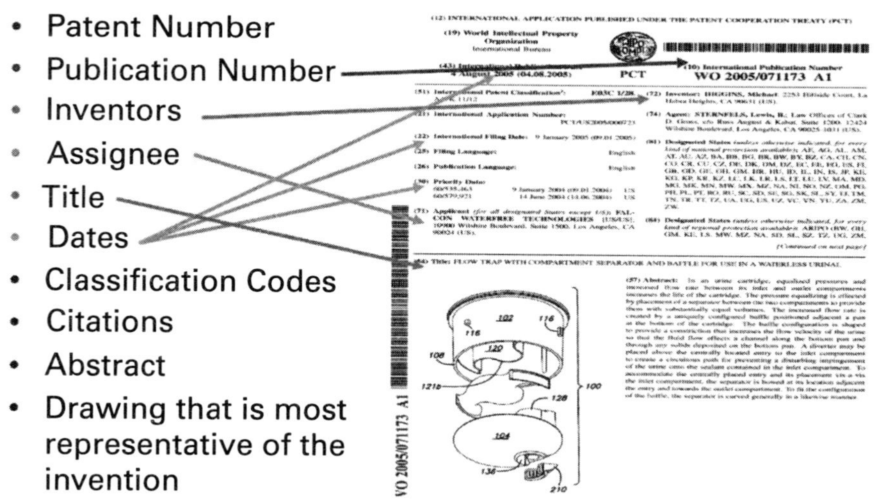

Figure 2. A typical front page of a patent application, and the information available contained therein.

Description" and "Examples". These may also be known in different ways, for example "Summary of the Invention" may otherwise be represented as "Brief Description" or "Object of the Invention", and so on. All of these sections combined are generally referred to as the specification. All these sections play a pivotal role in describing the invention in that they provide the definitions and descriptions of the terms given in the claims. For example the background provides a brief overview of the state-of-the-art in that particular technical field. Examples generally provide any experiments conducted and data therefrom that proves or enables the invention as claimed.

The specification is generally looked at to interpret the invention as claimed and also to determine the scope of invention. It is the primary source of definition and description and thus must be viewed first during interpretation, before any extraneous material such as dictionary or encyclopaedias.

CLAIMS

Claims are the most important part of a patent as they constitute the boundaries of the "rights" for the invention disclosed in the patent. Claims are the heart and soul of a patent in that they represent the scope of the invention. This is the enforceable part of a patent. They are sequentially numbered, and range from broad to narrow. Claims may be directed towards compositions, method of making, method of using, articles, products, systems, or product by process, and combinations thereof.

Claims are of two kinds: independent claims and dependent claims. Independent claims are generally the broadest in scope. They provide just the minimum elements necessary that differentiates the invention over existing prior art. Dependent claims, on the other hand, depend on one or more claims. The claim upon which a dependent claim depends may be an independent or a dependent claim. They generally narrow the scope of the invention as defined in the independent claims. They may also provide additional elements to add to the features given in the independent claim. When the dependent claim depends on more than one claim, it is referred to as a multiple dependent claim.

Some claims that depend on another claim may be treated as independent claims due to the manner in which it is worded. This is because the claim now provides a different scope of invention. For example, "A product comprising a composition made by the method of claim 1" is a typical "product by process" claim and may be considered independent claim for all practical purposes.

14

Patent Draft

Rachna Singh Puri,
Xellect IP Solutions, Bangalore
&
Malathi Lakshmikumaran,
Lakshmikumaran & Sridharan, Delhi

A granted patent gives the inventors or the applicant the right to exclude others from making, using, selling, offering for sale, or importing the invention. This exclusivity right is given by a jurisdiction for a limited period of time in exchange for FULL DISCLOSURE of the invention. The corollary to this statement is that the exclusivity rights can be asserted only for what has been disclosed. Anything not disclosed in a patent cannot be excluded by anyone. Hence nobody can stop anyone from making, using, selling, importing or offering for sale anything NOT disclosed in a patent document. This is an important point to be remembered while dealing with patent related matters.

The next level of detail to be considered is that even within a patent document, the exclusivity rights can be exercised for only what has been claimed, which means whatever is in the CLAIMS section of the patent document. We have already seen the various sections of a patent document. Among these different sections, the Claims section is considered to be the most critical part of the patent because only the matter mentioned in the Claims can be used to assert the exclusivity rights. All other sections of a patent application are generally considered to be in support of the Claims.

Thus, it can be seen that drafting a patent application is an important task, and has to be done with great care and caution. Badly drafted patent documents result in insufficient protection for an invention, or sometimes render the patent document invalid. Indeed, as we will see in the Chapter 17 on page 131 Search and Analyses of Patent Literature, 'insufficiency of disclosure' is grounds for rendering a patent invalid. Many times, a really great idea and the invention resulting therefrom has been rendered impotent in a marketplace for the applicant due to weakly drafted patents. The flip side of this story is that strong patents have resulted not only in strong protection and exclusivity rights for the applicant, but has also served as a source of extra revenue.

So let us go over the various sections of the patent again. Besides the front page contents which includes the Abstract, there are 'Technical Field', 'Background', 'Brief Description' or 'Summary', 'Detailed Description', 'Drawings' and the 'Claims'. As we have already seen, these section headers may be slightly different depending on the patent drafter, but essentially these sections will be present in any given patent document. Each of these sections has a specific role to play in a patent document, and they all have to work together to form a strong patent document.

The Background section deals with the state-of-the-art with respect to the present invention. In this section, the patent is supposed to provide a succinct overview of the problem being addressed, and the solutions already available, either in the market in the form of products, or in any of the references. References may include patent literature and non-patent literature. As will be pointed out in the Chapter 17 Search and Analyses chapter, patent literature contains substantially more technical information and data that is generally not covered in any other form of publication. So, preparation for a good patent document will start with a thorough literature search, with a special emphasis on patent literature, and then a summary of the key solutions from these references is provided in general terms in the Background section.

The patent, especially the Detailed Description, must CLEARLY describe the invention such that: (a) the written description must clearly allow a person of ordinary skill in the art to make and use the invention without "undue experimentation" and (b) the scope of enablement provided in the disclosure must be commensurate with the scope of the claims so as to prevent the applicant from claiming more than what he has invented. Thus, one cannot leave out a particular detail that is essential/critical to the working of the invention on the grounds that it is a trade secret. Different jurisdictions have enacted laws and guidelines that provide the clarity clause explicitly.

The courts in the USA apply the Wands factors to determine the enablement requirement: (In re Wands, 858 F.2d 731 (Fed. Cir. 1988)).

1. amount of experimentation necessary for those skilled in the art to apply and use the invention;
2. the amount of direction or guidance presented in the description to apply the invention;
3. the presence of working examples, such that it can effectively act as a bridge between the actual invention and the breadth of the claims. Even one may be sufficient in a given case;

4. the nature of the invention;
5. the state of the prior art, which can be used to fill in small gaps in the disclosure;
6. the relative skill of those in the art (this decides from whose perspective the description must be viewed);
7. the predictability or unpredictability of the art (For instance, chemistry and biotechnology is considered by courts in the to be inherently unpredictable); and
8. the breadth of the claims.

The weight to be accorded to each of these factors and their relevance in any given case is completely subjective. Further, these factors have been held not to be exhaustive and are only illustrative. A special mention ought to be made regarding the factor – predictability or unpredictability of the art. Case-laws indicate that when a particular art is considered unpredictable, there is a higher chance that the scope of the claims will more readily exceed the scope of enablement and be rejected as unduly broad. (The second level of enablement mentioned above.) This is plainly for the reason that the level of knowledge and research in that field may not be at a highly developed stage and thus, when only a single embodiment is claimed, claiming on a broader scope would not be allowed since it can be predicted that the invention will work equally well in the other embodiments claimed, but not disclosed. On the other hand, in predictable technologies, for instance, automobile engineering, suppose the embodiment disclosed is in a pedal system or a steering system in a four-wheeler, but the claim scope is broader and applies over all vehicles (a generic claim), it will still be allowed since any skilled person in that art can credibly predict that the invention will work equally well in other embodiments as well.

Next, the patent applicant must disclose the best mode of carrying out the invention, as was known at the time the application was filed. Thus, after an application has been filed, if the applicant continues to refine the invention, all subsequent discoveries may be pursued as additional patents. This requirement is designed to prevent a patentee from 'holding back' knowledge from the public, in effect maintaining part of the invention as a trade secret while protecting the whole under patent law. The 'best mode' description is not required by the EPC, where it is enough that the application includes at least one way of practising the invention.

As part of the enablement, providing as much experimental data to support the claims is advantageous, as this can only strengthen the patent. This is one of the reasons why an idea alone without any proper experiment data may not become a strong patent by itself. On the other hand, an idea that is well-thought out and experimented on, or at least backed by sufficient theoretical backing and calculations and simulations, will make for a stronger patent.

Another important aspect of the Specification is that it must also clearly define all the terms used in the patent document. Please note the use of the term Specification here – this is because definitions can be given anywhere in the patent document except the Claims. Generally, abstract is not a good place to provide definitions. The best place to provide proper definitions is in the Detailed Description section, although the Background section can also be used for this purpose. Anyone in the same field can generally understand the terms given, but in some instances, there may be ambiguity in the interpretations. The first place that will be looked into to resolve these ambiguities will be the patent document itself. In the absence of any particular definitions, the prevailing dictionary will be used to interpret the terms used. In many instances, there may be subtle but significant differences between the dictionary meaning and the actual "use" meaning. This difference may prove detrimental in such situations. To avoid this situation, the best practice is to define each and every term critical to novelty and understanding of the invention.

Claims

As already mentioned, claims are by far the most important part of a patent. As one court succinctly suggested, "[T]he name of the game is the claim." (See In re Hiniker Co., 150 F.3d 1362 (Fed. Cir. 1998)). Claims describe the metes and bounds of the patentee's right. Whenever a patentee wishes to secure his / her right by filing infringement suits, the first step that is undertaken is to analyze the claims and verify if the alleged infringing device or process falls within the scope of the claim. It is well-recognized in patent law that claims fulfill two functions: (a) they define the scope of the patentee's right; and (b) the public notice function – the claims provide public notice to those in the field as to the scope of the right to exclude others from practicing the invention and therefore warn those in the field as to the area that they must not interfere with. As is evident, these two functions are merely two sides of the same coin and are inter-related.

For this reason, patent law generally mandates certain minimum standards for claims. In the USA, the claims must particularly point out and distinctly claim the subject-matter which the applicant regards as his invention. Similarly, Indian law requires that the claim(s) define the scope of the invention for which protection is claimed. Under the EPC, claims are required to define the matter for which protection is sought, and must be clear and concise.

There can be more than one claim for a patent, but they must be of different scopes (so that they are not redundant) and must be numbered consecutively. Generally, the Claims section begins with "I/We claim", or may simply start with the title "Claims" that appears just once before all the claims and that each claim is written in a single sentence. The following is exemplary of a well-defined claim: (*See* Landis on Mechanics of Patent Claim Drafting, § 45, *V-2)

"I claim

1. A resistor, which comprises:
   (a) a ceramic core;
   (b) a coating of carbon on the ceramic core; and
   (c) a strip of conductive metal at each end of the ceramic core in electrical contact with the coating of carbon."

When we deconstruct this claim, we may divide it into three parts:

Preamble

This is the introductory phrase to the claim and generally indicates the field of the invention. For instance, in the above claim, "A resistor..." is the preamble. It introduces the reader to the subject-matter of the invention. In terms of administrative procedure, it helps the Patent office in classifying the applications and conducting prior art searches. Sometimes, the preamble may include intended purposes, general prior art elements etc., e.g. "A resistor used in a generator ..."

Transitional Phrase/Connector

As the name suggests, this is the phrase or word that connects the preamble to the body of the claim. In the above claim, the word 'comprising' is the transition phrase. Common transition phrases are 'which comprises' or 'comprising', 'including', 'consisting of', 'having' and 'consisting essentially of.' The phrase 'comprising' is considered 'open ended'. Therefore, an invention claimed as "comprising A & B" will be infringed by a device having elements A, B & C. Whereas, 'consisting of' is interpreted as 'close ended' and limits the scope of the claim exclusively to the elements given in the body. Taking the previous example, the device with an additional element will be held as not infringing the patent. 'Consisting essentially of' is somewhere in the middle of these extremes and allows for the claim scope to include additional elements that do not play any significant role (do not materially affect the characteristics of the device or process). The other transition phrases can have varied effects depending on the context.

Body

As a general rule, that part of the claim that follows the transitional phrase is the body of the claim. It recites the elements or parts of the invention that the patentee wishes to exercise his rights over. Sometimes, the elements or parts of the invention are also referred to as inventive features, or limitations. Clear and intelligible wordings must be used to describe these elements of the invention.

A simple technique that can be used to draft claims would be to list the preamble and the elements of the invention first. Subsequently, the role of each element is taken into account as to the working of the invention, to leave behind only the most essential features required for the working of the invention. At this point, care must be taken to avoid reading upon anything already disclosed in the prior art. There must be a clear differentiation from the prior art as well to prove both novelty and inventiveness. The same step of "minimization" must then be performed on the preamble as well. Then, each of the elements left behind are to be represented in a generalized form. Care must again be used to ensure that each of the elements in its generalized form is capable of interacting with each other in the manner that is envisioned in the invention. This exercise when done diligently will provide a claim that is broad in scope.

Typology of Claims

Claims may be of various types: *independent*, *dependent* and *multiple dependent* claims. A claim is said to be independent when it is complete in itself and stands alone. All the elements are recited within the same claim and does not refer back to or draw limitations from other claims. The claim recited above (resistor) is an example of an independent claim. Dependent claims are those that do not stand alone and depend or draw the limitations of another independent claim or another dependent claim. For instance, the following is a dependent claim to the independent claim written above referring to a resistor:

> "2. A resistor as claimed in claim 1, wherein the said coating of carbon is deposited by the process comprising: ..."

Thus claim 2 adds one other element or limitation to the invention in claim 1. By definition, the dependent claim incorporates all the limitations of the independent claim. But the vice versa is not true. Dependent claims are thus narrower in scope than the parent independent claim. When a claim is dependent on more than one claim, then it is a multiple dependent claim. This multiple dependency is referred to in alternative language. E.g. "An apparatus as claimed in claim 1 *or* 2....." as opposed to "An apparatus as claimed in claim 1 *and* 2....."

Claim Formats

Legislations do not mandate any particular format for writing claims. So long as the claim is clear & concise, it is irrelevant as to how they are written, i.e. their structure, sequencing and words used. Over the years however, various methods of drafting or writing claims have been developed to suit particular types of technologies and inventions and today they are accepted in the field as standardized claim formats even by the courts. Each "claim format", as is generally referred to, has its own advantages and limitations. Generally, in a given patent, various claim formats are strategically used in conjunction to provide optimum protection to the rights of the patentee. The following are brief explanations of the important ones:

1. ***Jepson Claims***: The *Jepson* format is one of the oldest claim formats. A rough variation of this exists in the EPC as well, and is generally referred to as "Two-Part Claim". Under statutory rules of the USA, a Jepson claim assumes the following structure:

    a. A preamble comprising a general description of all the elements or steps of the claimed combination which are conventional or known in prior art;
    b. A transitional phrase such as "wherein the improvement comprises," and
    c. Those elements, steps, and/or relationships which constitute that portion of the claimed combination which the applicant considers as the new or improved portion.

Since the preamble in this case explains the elements of the invention at a systemic level, as an exception to the general rule, the preamble in such claims constitutes a limitation or element of the invention. It is generally employed where the patentee has used a new element or component in conjunction with an already existing device such that the combination is a novel one. When written in this format, everything written prior to the transition phrase (in the preamble) is presumed to be admitted as prior art. The following claim, taken from the case of (*Rowe v. Dror, 112 F.3d 473* (*1997*)), is a good example of this format:

> "1. In a balloon angioplasty catheter of the type comprising a catheter body and a balloon positioned along the length of the catheter body, said balloon including means for remotely inflating and deflating said balloon; *the improvement comprising*:
>
> (a) a plurality of microcapsules on the exterior of said balloon, each of said microcapsules carrying a drug or combination of drugs for treatment or diagnostics within a body lumen when the said catheter is positioned and inflated therewithin such that the drug or drugs may be released from said microcapsules."

Thus, herein, the applicant makes an admission that catheter body, a balloon positioned along the length of the catheter body, and means for remotely inflating and deflating said the balloon are known in prior art.

The only invention/improvement that he claims is the use of microcapsules embedded on the balloon carrying a drug which is released whenever the balloon is inflated. Further, the invention relates to only an angioplasty catheter as opposed to any general purpose catheter since this element though mentioned only in the preamble acts as a claim limitation.

2. ***Markush Claims*:** When the invention relates to the use of chemical different compounds or processes which result in the same result, then instead of using different claims for each of these alternates, *Markush* format allows us to cover all these alternatives within one claim. The *Markush* format developed due to the reason that sometimes the relevant art does not have generic expressions or groups to collate the various alternatives. For instance, Fluorine, Chlorine, Bromine etc. are under the head 'Halogens'; but, Hydrogen and Methane do not fall under any generic group. It seems unreasonable to allow someone to have a single claim using halogens, but not allow someone to claim using Hydrogen and Methane in a single claim only because there is paucity in scientific terminology.

This format is generally employed in chemical cases, though not necessarily. The following is a good example: (*Taken from U.S. Patent No. 3234948, Cheese-filter Cigarette, Stuart M. Stebbings, February 15, 1966*)

> "A cigarette filter according to claim 1, in which the cheese comprises grated particles of cheese *selected from the group consisting of* Parmesan, Romano, Swiss and cheddar cheeses."

The italicized phrase is the key characteristic of Markush claims. For a group of members to be used in a Markush format, the members of the group share a common utility and a substantial structural feature that is essential to that utility. To explain this better, the members of a group that are being attempted to be clubbed in a Markush group have at least one common property that is, essential to the utility. Note that 'consisting' and not 'comprising' is used, otherwise, the claim would cover even those alternatives not mentioned, thereby making the scope indefinite.

3. ***Means-plus-function Claims*:** (§ 112, paragraph 6) This format has a very controversial beginning. It was initially struck down by the US Supreme Court for being ambiguous and indefinite in scope. This was legislatively overruled and this format is the one of the few formats which now has legislative sanction. This format can be employed only in combination claims where the invention involves a combination of various elements. For instance: (*Taken from Halliburton Oil*

Well Cementing Co. v. Walker, 329 U.S. 1 (1946) where such claims were originally struck down).

"In an apparatus for determining the location of an obstruction in a well having therein a string of assembling tubing sections interconnected with each other by coupling collars, *means communicating with the said well for creating a pressure impulse* in the said well, *echo receiving means including a pressure responsive device exposed to the said well for receiving pressure impulses* from the well and for measuring the lapse of time between the creation of the impulse and the arrival at said receiving means of the echo from said obstruction, *and means associated with the said pressure responsive device for tuning* said receiving means to the frequency of echoes from the tubing collars of the said tubing sections to clearly distinguish the echoes from said couplings from each other."

Note that the use of the phrase 'means' is characteristic of this format; no structure for the said elements is given. Instead, they are defined by their function. This means plus function claims use functional language at the exact point of novelty. And for the purposes of interpreting this claim, the claim is defined to embody only structures that are described in the description part of the specification.

However, the patent application must clearly provide different means that are known for implementing the function. This kind of language is usually shied away from by many attorneys due to its possible indefinite nature.

4. ***Product-by-process Claims***: In this format, the product or at least one element of the invention is defined by reciting the process of fabricating or preparing it. The claim still remains of the product and the case, the novelty and non-obviousness requirements is to be judged on the product only.

Similar to *Markush* formats, even this format arose as a matter of necessity. Suppose, the product to be claimed is a building material prepared by a process other than the conventional one. The material thus prepared shows enhanced mechanical strength, but the applicant is unable to identify the structural differences resulting in this property. In such cases, it is reasonable to allow the applicant to identify the product through the process.

"I claim

1. A process for treating a surface of a polyethylene article to increase its receptivity to printing ink, which comprises: exposing the surface of the article to a saturated solution of sodium dichromate in acid.

2. A polyethylene article having a surface treated in accordance with the process of claim 1"

(Source: *Landis on Mechanics of Patent Claim Drafting, § 42 & 46, *IV-17 & *V-9*)

With respect to the above product claim, the process of manufacturing it will now be a claim limitation. Thus anyone who produces the same product through a different process will not infringe the claim.

5. ***Swiss-Type Claims*:** A Swiss-type claim or "Swiss type of use claim" is a claim intended to cover the second or subsequent medical use (or indication) of a known substance or composition. This is a special situation wherein the original compound in question is already known, so it cannot be novel or non-obvious or inventive. However, the new use makes it novel in some manner, but the use is in a medical use. As we have already seen in the 'Patentable Subject Matter' chapter, medical treatments are generally not patentable in many jurisdictions, such as EP and India. Thus, the structure of the claim that appeases the EPO guidelines and the pharmaceutical industries in EP is as follows: "Use of compound X in the manufacture of a medication for the treatment of Y". This claim cannot be allowed in India, as Section 3(d) explicitly excludes such inventions as not patentable. The name "Swiss-type claims" arose because such claims had first been allowed in Switzerland.

6. ***Beauregard Claims*:** In United States patent law, a Beauregard claim is a claim to an article of manufacture embodied as a computer-readable medium and instructions, named after decision In re Beauregard (53 F.3d 1583 Fed. Cir. 1995). Beauregard claims involve a computer-readable medium such as a storage device, such as a floppy disk or CD, containing a set of instructions that causes a computer to perform a process.

Coming back to claims in general, it is a good strategy to have claims must also be drafted with varying scopes, while ensuring that the unity of invention is still preserved. The various scopes of an invention are as follows: Composition, Method of Making a composition, Method of Using a composition, Article, Apparatus, System, and a Product. So, if the core of the invention is a composition or a method of implementation, or an apparatus, then claims must also be drawn to the other scopes, as is deemed possible by the invention.

Claims are also drafted such that it is geared towards something that can be seen in public view. This is generally towards a composition, an article a product, a system etc. This is done so that if anyone else, without the applicant's permission, makes, uses, sells, or imports the invention as claimed, the infringer can be easily caught "red-handed". A claim towards something that is not directly seen in public view – such as a method of manufacture, which is generally done within private premises – is considered less powerful, when put head-to-head with the other more powerful claims. But this does not mean that such claims should not be drafted. Such claims have their merits and uses, and must be drafted to offer the breadth of coverage that an invention deserves.

Patent Drafting is a skilful art that uses the several million words of the language available to the drafter and utilize these words to ensure that the invention is captured adequately. Subsequently, using these carefully chosen words, the rest of the world is put on notice about the exclusivity gained by the applicant. Most inventors find drafting of patent applications a difficult task. However, inventors are the most capable of reviewing a patent application as drafted to ensure that it adequately covers the invention. Inventors also have the burden of providing direction of extending and broadening the scope of the invention in the patent drafting by giving appropriate directions to the patent drafter. This is something that all inventors and even business managers and leaders can and ought to do.

15

Filing Patent Applications

Once a patent application has been drafted, the next step is to file the patent application with the appropriate one or more patent offices. It must be clearly understood that there is no way of making only one application for a patent and get a "world" patent granted. Such a facility does not exist as of today. Indeed such a facility does not exist for any form of intellectual property, as of today. In all the forms of intellectual property, to be able to acquire exclusivity rights in a particular jurisdiction, it is necessary to file an application in each individual jurisdiction and get it granted by that respective authority. The system may evolve in different ways in the future to enable simplification of this process, but it doesn't exist today.

However, there exists a useful mechanism whereby a single patent application can be filed with an international organization, World Intellectual Property Organization, WIPO, from where one can get a fair idea of whether the patent application has a good chance to get past the four gates of patent viz. statutory patentable subject matter, novelty, inventive step or non-obviousness, utility or industrial applicability. Subsequently, the process of filing the patent application in each jurisdiction has to be undergone.

Patent Co-operation Treaty, referred to as PCT is a treaty signed by more than 160 countries worldwide. Each signatory country is also referred to as a Convention Country. This is a useful treaty in that a patent application made in one country can be easily referred to in another country.

WHO CAN FILE PATENT APPLICATIONS?

Patent applications can typically be filed by a patent agent or a patent attorney. A patent agent is a person who is qualified to act in all matters related to patent law with the respective patent offices. It is very important to note that each jurisdiction has its own set of qualified patent agents. A qualified patent agent in one jurisdiction cannot work with any other jurisdiction. Patent agents are also qualified to handle matters ONLY with the patent offices. To deal with matters in a court, a patent agent must also be qualified as a patent attorney, which requires a full-fledged law degree. In Europe, someone who is qualified as a patent agent is also referred to as a patent attorney. Due to the similarity of terminology, and the casual use of these titles by different jurisdictions, confusion may arise when attempting to obtain services from a professional in the jurisdiction. Thus, a quick cursory study of the requirements in a jurisdiction must be done before approaching anyone there.

In India, an inventor, as long as the inventor is an Indian citizen, is allowed to file patent applications, either on his/her own behalf, or on behalf of the applicant. In U.S., interestingly, only the inventors can apply for a patent application. So the forms and procedures involved there are all designed such that the inventors file for a patent protection, and then subsequently assign it to the interested party, such as their employees or organizations they belong to. This is one of the reasons why the organizations are more often referred to as Assignees in U.S. In U.S. also, registered patent agents and patent attorneys exist who can act on behalf of the inventors, but the inventors have to still assign the invention to the appropriate parties.

PROVISIONAL SPECIFICATION OR PROVISIONAL PATENT APPLICATION

Whenever an invention is in an early developmental stage and there are many more experiments planned, and the inventor or the applicant feels there is a need to obtain a very early priority date, then filing a provisional specification is useful. India and U.S. provides such a facility. It is referred to as a provisional specification in India, while in U.S. it is called provisional patent application. A provisional specification contains some details about the invention as envisioned by the inventor, and does not require claims or abstract. In India, the provisional specification is accompanied with a Form 1, Form 2 and the appropriate fees, which is INR 4000/-. The fee for a provisional patent application in U.S. is USD 220/-. There is no requirement for the declaration as to inventorship or assignment of deed. A provisional specification is filed in order to obtain the earlier priority date, and is not enforceable at any point by itself. Provisional specification is also never published by itself.

India has 4 patent offices in Mumbai, Chennai, Delhi and Kolkata. Each of these offices has a set of states within their territorial limits. Any organization, entity or individual wishing to apply for a patent application must apply to the relevant patent office associated with the place of work or address for correspondence.

Please note that in India, the fees for an Individual or Natural Person(s) are lower than those for Entities such as any Organizations. Similarly, U.S. differentiates between Small Entities and Large Entities. As a thumb rule, it can be understood that Small Entities are any educational institutions, Not-For-Profit Organizations, or For-Profit Organizations that have less than 50 employees. But the appropriate section of the law must be consulted before arriving at this conclusion. All the fees given here are for large organizations.

CLAIMING PRIORITY

Any patent application can claim the priority of a previously filed provisional patent specification, or a non-provisional patent application or a complete specification or a PCT filing. The effect of claiming priority is that the priority date for the invention is the original date of filing of the application it is claiming priority to. This helps because any reference that is considered novelty destroying – also referred to by the practitioners in the field as PRIOR ART – for such applications has to be publicly available earlier to the priority date. Figure 3 gives a line diagram illustration of determination of priority date.

Given this, it must be noted that a non-provisional patent application or a complete specification cannot claim priority infinitely. Once a provisional specification has been filed, there is a twelve-month limit within which priority to this provisional specification can be made by filing a Non-provisional Application. At the expiry of twelve months, it is not possible to claim the priority, baring some really exceptional circumstances.

Similarly, priority can be claimed from a patent application filed in a convention country while filing for a patent application in another country. The time limit for such filing is 12 months. This means that once a patent appli-

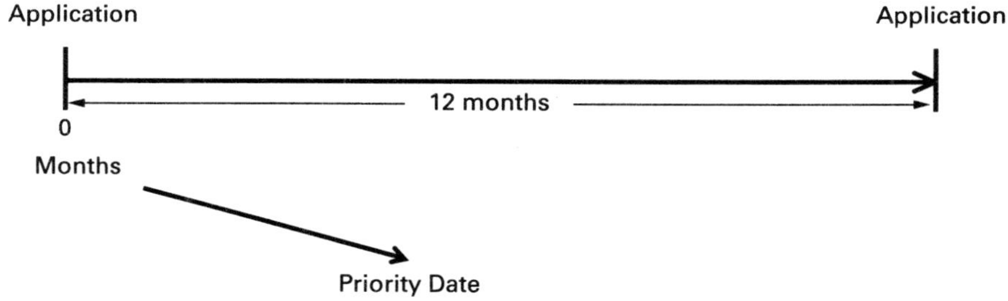

Figure 3. Line diagram illustration of determination of priority date.

cation filed in India, before the expiry of one year, patent applications have to be filed in all the convention countries that the applicant is interested in.

Further, a PCT application (see later) can act as a priority document as well. The time limit for being able to take priority from a PCT application is 30 months or 31 months (depending on the country) from the filing date. However, if the PCT application itself takes priority from a different earlier filed application – whether a provisional or a non-provisional – then the time limit is 30 or 31 months from the priority date.

COMPLETE SPECIFICATION OR NON-PROVISIONAL PATENT APPLICATION

All patent applications can be filed for protection anywhere in the world without prejudice. Each jurisdiction has its own requirements and fee structure. Once these requirements are met, then the patent application can be filed there and get it in a condition to be granted. But one key requirement that any jurisdiction will typically be contained within their local law and/or statutes is that if an invention has been made within that particular jurisdiction, then a patent application has to be filed there first before applying elsewhere in the world. This means that if an invention has been made in India first, the inventors have to file for patent protection in India first before applying for patent protection in U.S., Europe, Japan etc. Alternately, a permission for filing a patent application outside the jurisdiction may be obtained from the respective patent office, and then a patent application can be filed anywhere else in the world. Thus, for an invention made in India, a permission can be obtained from the Controller of Patents in India to be filed outside India first.

India

A complete patent application, or as referred to in India as a Complete Specification, comprises at least the following documents: the patent application which includes all the sections of a patent document, Form 1 Application for a Patent, Form 2 Complete Specification, Form 3 Statement and Undertaking regarding foreign filing details in respect of same invention, Form 5 Declaration as to Inventorship, and Form 26 power of attorney, if the services of a patent agent or a patent attorney is made use of.

The fees for a complete specification is INR 4000/-, for which the applicant is allowed to file a patent application having 30 pages and 10 claims. For each extra page, it costs INR 400/- per page, and for each extra claim over 10, it costs INR 800/- per claim. Further, a Request for Examination has to be filed using Form 18, along with a fee of INR 10,000/-.

U.S.

In U.S. the Complete Specification is filed along with a Transmittal Form, Oath or Declaration, a Power of Attorney (if using the services of a patent agent), and an Information Disclosure Statement or IDS. The IDS contains all the references that the inventor is aware of and considers it relevant to the claims of the patent application. This is an obligation unique to the U.S. system. The obligation to bring references to the notice of the U.S. Patent Office continues upto the grant of a patent application. This is a serious obligation, and failure to do so may result in rendering the patent application invalid.

The fees for filing a patent application includes the basic filing fee of USD 330/-. The basic filing fee provides upto 3 independent claims and a total of 20 claims. For each additional independent claim, USD 220/- per claim is charged, while each additional claim greater than 20, a fee of USD 52/- is charged. Further a search fee of USD 540/- and an examination fee of USD 110/- has to be paid.

PCT

Patent Co-operation Treaty, commonly referred to as PCT is a very useful mechanism to file patent applications, and obtain a reasonable search report and an opinion related to the granting ability of the patent application as filed. To this end, there are a few terminologies that need to be clearly understood. A Receiving Office (RO) is a patent office which is capable of receiving and handling PCT applications. The choice of RO depends on the nationality of the inventors and/or the applicant. Typically, the country where the invention was made becomes the RO for any patent applications therefrom. In situations where multiple inventors from different countries come up with an invention, then the applicant's country determines the choice of RO. Alternately, the RO can also be the International Bureau (IB), which is located in Switzerland. This is generally neutral in nature.

Once the RO is decided, the International Search Authority (ISA) must also be decided upon. The responsibility of the ISA is to provide a search report referred to as International Search Report (ISR) for the claims of a patent application. The ISA also provides an opinion on the patentability of the claims of the patent application, which is referred to as International Preliminary Examination Report (IPER). Currently, the ISAs available to an applicant are as follows: (the two alphabets in capitals within the brackets indicate the code by which they are referred to)

1. Austrian Patent Office (AT).
2. Australian Patent Office (AU).
3. Canadian Intellectual Property Office (CA).

4. State Intellectual Property Office of the People's Republic of China (CN).
5. European Patent Office (EP).
6. Spanish Patent and Trademark Office (ES).
7. National Board of Patents and Registration of Finland (FI).
8. Japan Patent Office (JP).
9. Korean Intellectual Property Office (KR).
10. Federal Service for Intellectual Property, Patents and Trademarks (Russian Federation) (RU).
11. Swedish Patent and Registration Office (SE).
12. United States Patent and Trademark Office (US).
13. Nordic Patent Institute (XN).

Each RO is also associated with a set of ISAs, and so depending on the choice of an RO, an applicant has only those ISAs to choose from. Each ISA has its own fee structure as well. The PCT authorities maintain the same level of quality among all the ISAs, but due to some traditional approaches and a preference towards a particular ISA by some patent practitioners this also factors during the choice of an ISA.

For a PCT filing, besides the patent application containing all the sections, the following paper-work is also required for filing:

- Request that includes
    - Inventor(s)' Details
    - Applicant(s), if different from Inventors
    - Agent/Representative Details
    - Title of the Invention
    - Claim to Priority, if any
    - Designated States
    - Choice of International Search Authority
- Power of Attorney (if the application is made through a patent agent)

Designated States means those countries or jurisdictions that the applicant intends to file after the PCT phase is completed. The fee for filing depends on the choice of RO, Designated States, ISA, the number of pages of the patent application.

Europe

European Patent Office (EPO) is an interesting situation. EPO is part of the European Patent Organization (having the confusing similar acronym EPO, but it is generally distinguished by the use of EPOrg), but is not bound to the political entity i.e. European Union EU. There are currently 35 contracting states that are affiliated to the EPO. A patent can be filed with the EPO, it undergoes examination according to the European Patent Convention (EPC) and if found appropriate to do so, gets granted. However, this patent as such is not enforceable in any of the countries. Subsequently, the patents have to be "registered" in each of the contracting states, with the payment of the necessary fees, and providing appropriate translation. The registration process is one of administrative in nature, and the patent as such does not undergo a subsequent examination. These registered patents are then enforceable in that particular state.

Alternately, a patent application can be filed in each individual state initially, and then subsequently, an application can be filed with the EPO. In this case, even if the original patent application is examined, the EPO will conduct its own search and examination to determine if the patent is worthy of a grant.

Each individual state will have some nuances with respect to the paper work and law, although, to a large extent, this has been standardized by the EPO. The papers required for filing with the EPO are as follows: Request that contains Inventor(s) Details, Applicant Details, Claiming of Priority, if any, Representation by an agent or attorney, Power of Attorney and the Complete Patent Application. The fees for filing includes several headers, and are given in Table 9.

POST-FILING PROCESS

Once the patent application package is deemed complete by the respective patent office or the PCT RO, then a filing receipt is generated, which will give the unique identifying number for the patent application. Subsequently, the patent office will check to see if any errors or any portions of the application that are missing. The Chapter 16 on page 123 patent

Table 9 Filing Fees in EPO

Assignment	Amount in Euros	
Filing Fees	Paper Filing 180	Online Filing 100
	For 15 Claims, Euros 200 per claim in excess of 16 claims	
Designation Fee for each Contracting State designated	85 Designation fees being deemed paid for all contracting states upon payment of seven times the amount of this fee = 595	
Search Fee	1050	
Examination Fee	1405	

prosecution deals with this aspect in greater detail. At the end of 18 months from the priority date of the patent application, it will be published in the publication as designated by the appropriate patent office. Typically, it is on the patent office website, but it may also be in the gazette or some other publication. EPO, U.S., India publish the patent applications on their corresponding websites. Thus, this published application becomes prior art and can be used as a reference for any studies, or future inventions.

For the purposes of enforcement, a published application is as good as an enforceable patent, unless the patent office explicitly states that it has been rejected or abandoned. Section 11a, Paragraph (7) of the Indian Patents Act, 1970 states that "On and from the date of publication of the application for patent and until the date of grant of a patent in respect of such application, the applicant shall have the like privileges and rights as if a patent for the invention had been granted on the date of publication of the application ..." However, the publication of a patent application only enables the applicant to put any infringers on notice, and cannot be actually used to start any infringement proceedings until the grant of the patent. Section 11A, Paragraph (7) of the Indian Patents Act, 1970 further states that "... Provided that the applicant shall not be entitled to institute any proceedings for infringement until the patent has been granted."

A generalized overview of the processes involved after the filing of a patent application is given in a flow chart in Figure 4. Oppositions or Invalidations are discussed in greater detail in the Chapter 17 on page 131 Search and Analyses of Patent Literature.

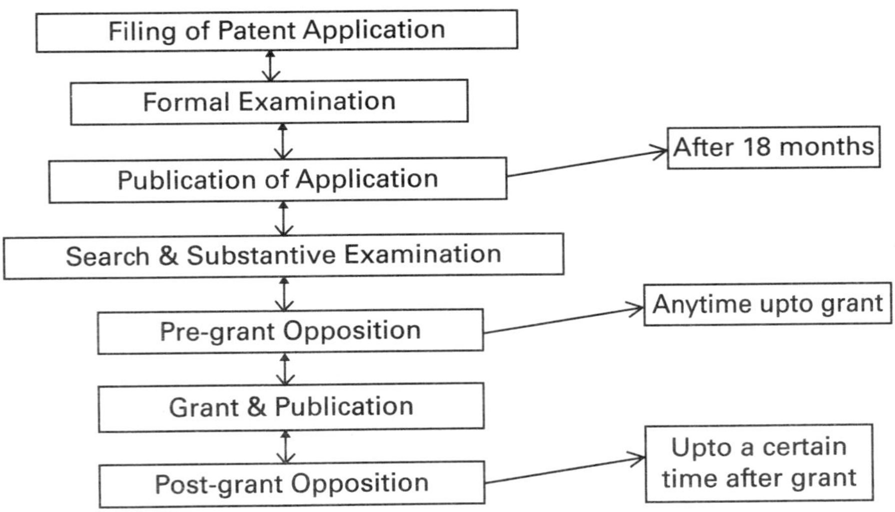

Figure 4. Broad overview of the processes involved after the filing of a patent application.

Any inventor can easily be part of the process of procuring the exclusivity rights up to this point. This includes the ideation, identifying the problem, coming up with a suitable solution, and experimentation, followed by patent preparation, and filing the papers with the appropriate patent office. After this, the whole situation takes a tricky turn and generally, unless the inventor is a patent professional or a business manager, the whole matter is generally out of his/her hands. Prosecution requires skill, patience, experience and intricate knowledge of the patenting system to move the patent application from a mere published application to a granted patent form. Subsequently, any enforcement, infringement and other related proceedings are in the hands of a skilled attorney. Any business dealings such as licensing or selling or assigning, or even abandoning by non-payment of maintenance fees is in the hands of a business manager. But on several occasions, the inventors' assistance is sought for all these situations.

16

Patent Prosecution

Patent application is filed for an invention that stemmed from an idea in order to solve a problem with a technical solution. It so happens that despite the technical nature of everything involved here, a patent application is full of words. Words are subject to interpretations, and will acquire different meanings depending on the context and situation. Thus, even though the patent application is well written, but due to differing interpretations, the patent application may be viewed as being unpatentable. Mind you, this difference arises due to perfectly reasonable circumstances and situations, and there is nothing right or wrong about one person having a different interpretation of a set of words from another person's interpretation.

Given this knowledge, the responsibility largely lies with the patent drafter to ensure that such differences in interpretations do not arise. This can be done by giving proper definitions and using the appropriate words. But this is a difficult task, especially given the time allotted for such exercises. Thus, the drafter uses the best available words at his/her disposal and then proceeds to file the application with the patent office.

The patent office comprises a whole lot of Examiners whose designated job is to examine patent applications to see if they are worthy of being granted. Examiners are generally trained and knowledgeable about the technical field they are assigned to. So, in principle, they are of one skilled in the art in that particular field of invention.

The Examiner receives the patent application and is ready to grant patent applications as long as they fulfill the 4 criteria viz. the invention must be one of statutory patentable matter, novel, inventive or non-obvious and useful or industrially applicable.

The Examiner's first task is to ensure that the patent application package is complete, and no paper work has gone missing. If something is seen to be missing or the package is found to be in any way incomplete, then the

Examiner notifies the applicant about it immediately, and gives the applicant a certain time limit within which to respond to complete the package.

Generally, the time given for completing the application package is very less, often times only up to one month from the date the communication was mailed by the Patent Office. It must be stated that there is a possibility that one can overcome any delays and consequent non-adherence to prescribed deadlines as long as there is a good reason for the delay. Overcoming delays is also typically associated with fees.

Then, the Examiner reads the patent application carefully to understand the invention as claimed and described. The Examiner will then ensure that the subject matter of the patent application does not fall within the purview of any one of the non-patentable subject matter according to the law of the jurisdiction. It must be mentioned here that the Examiner will always take it that whatever is given in the patent application is true and valid unless he has conclusive evidence to the contrary. Thus, any experimental details, data, etc. will not be in any way verified by the Examiner, unless there is some other publication or reference which states facts to the contrary.

A thorough search is conducted by the Examiner to see what else has been published and known in this field. This will then assist the Examiner in making up a report regarding the patentability of the claims of the patent application. The report given by different patent offices go by various names and are of slightly different scopes. The Indian Patent Office provides a First Examination Report FER, which gives the details of the references considered for the patentability of the invention as claimed and the reasons why the claims are being rejected. The European Patent Office provides a Search Report, which is also a listing of references considered, but the references are classified as being closely relevant or just serve as a good background material for the patent application being considered. For more details on the classification of references in a search report, please see Chapter 13 on Patent Contents. Subsequently an opinion on the patentability of the claims in the patent application is provided upon request. PCT follows a similar procedure also. In U.S., the response from the patent office is called an Office Action, wherein the reasons for rejecting the claims are given in a detailed manner.

The rejections of claims are usually on the basis of lack of novelty or lack of inventive step, or in U.S., obviousness. The appropriate sections and articles of the law may also be quoted in the rejection. Generally, the Examiner will state that the invention claimed has been "anticipated" by a particular reference. Alternately, the Examiner might state that the "invention is not considered novel in the light of a particular reference, as evidenced by <line number>, <column number>". Rejections may also be on the basis of lack of clarity of the patent invention, lack of utility (in U.S.) or industrial applicability. Several sections of laws or the rules for implementing the laws in each of the jurisdictions actually delineate the clarity aspect. It is worthwhile stating here that rarely has a patent application gone through the scrutiny of an Examiner without a rejection of some sort or the other.

Rejected claims may be independent claims or dependent claims. Whenever a claim is rejected, any claim depending on the rejected claim is also considered rejected.

Finally, the Examiner will also usually provide some guidelines for making the application allowable. The Examiner will also indicate the timeline for response by the applicant.

As mentioned before, most of these rejections are based on the interpretations by the Examiner assigned the task of examining the patent applications. This may be unsatisfactory to the applicant. So, the applicant is allowed a chance to explain that why the Examiner's version of interpretation is wrong, then provide the applicant's version of the interpretations in a properly formatted response. The interpretation must be substantiated by some strong evidence, preferably from within the patent application itself.

Typically, if more than one reference is used to reject the claims of a patent application, then the response must address each of the reference individually as to why the applicant doesn't consider it to be relevant or different from his/her claims. Figure 5 gives an outline of the steps involved in the prosecution of patent applications. This broadly resembles the steps given in Figure 4, with an extra level of detail with regards to the nature of rejections also given here.

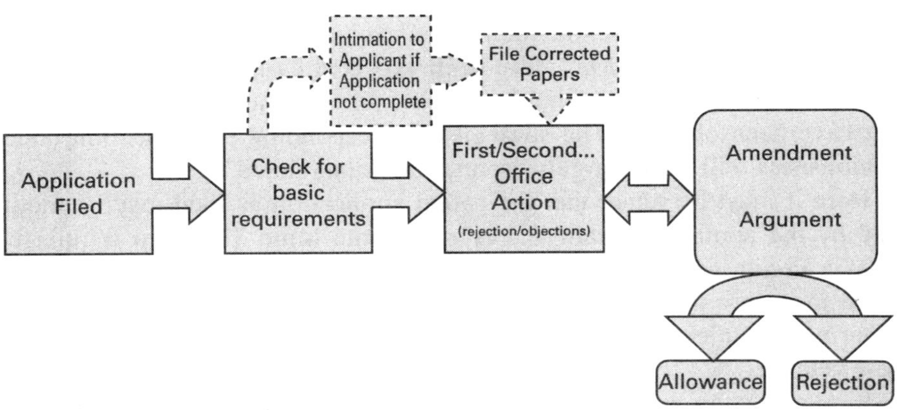

Figure 5. Overview of processes involved in the Prosecution of a Patent Application.

GUIDELINES TO HANDLE A REJECTION BASED ON ANTICIPATION

A claim is anticipated only if **each and every element** as set forth in the claim is found, either expressly or inherently described, in **a single prior art** reference. The elements of the claims in the patent application are interpreted by the examiner **in light of the specification and prosecution history**, and identify the corresponding elements disclosed in the allegedly anticipating reference. Further, the prior art found by the Examiner must be "enabling".

The prior art must first be scrutinized thoroughly to ensure that each of the conditions are met. Any deviation from any one of the conditions can be used as a point of argument in the response.

GUIDELINES TO HANDLE REJECTION BASED ON OBVIOUSNESS

For obviousness or inventive step related rejections, the prior art references must **teach or suggest all the claim limitations**. There should be a **suggestion or motivation**, either in the references themselves or in the knowledge generally available to one of ordinary skill in the art, to modify the reference or to combine reference teachings. The two points are generally referred to as the TSM Test – Teaching, Suggestion, Motivation to combine or modify references. **A reasonable expectation of success** must be available in the references or can be reasonably inferred from the references. Another aspect to bear in mind is that the claimed invention in the patent application must be **considered as a whole**. Further, a patentable invention may lie in the **identification of a source of a problem**, and not the solution for the problem itself. In many instances, once a problem has been identified, the solution becomes obvious, but that doesn't negate the patentability of an invention. Also, when teachings of two or more **prior art references conflict**, the references may not be combinable. Finally, any results which would not have been expected by those skilled in the art or are considered as surprising is strong evidence that the invention would not have been obvious. The strategies for responding to a rejection under obviousness will hinge largely around the points noted.

Here it must be stated that the patent application as filed may be modified by the applicant within a prescribed time limit. This step is referred to as a Preliminary Amendment, or simply Amendment. But care must be taken to ensure that the amended specification does not add anything new in terms of subject matter, but only reiterates or clarifies the matter in this new version.

Similarly, after a rejection, the applicant is allowed to amend the claims to better suit it for grant. This may be done as an alternative to arguing one's position with the Examiner. It just may make more political and business sense to amend the claims and get the patent application granted. Every time any part of the patent specification is amended, the amended portions must be clearly pointed out by appropriate striking out and underlining, or in some such manner. The amendment must also be substantiated in a separate letter as to the reasons for amending, the nature of the amendment, and any other details associated with this action. Once again, it is worth reiterating that NO NEW SUBJECT MATTER MAY BE ADDED during amendment. Often times, amendments may be associated with a fee.

After the response has been recorded with the patent office, the Examiner will then weigh the arguments and/or any amendments and will provide with the patent office's position towards the same. This may be:

- acceptance of argument or amendment thus resulting in allowance;
- that the Examiner holds ground and doesn't consider the arguments or amendments given by the applicant as persuasive, and hence give a final rejection.

After a **final rejection**, the applicant may:

– **abandon** the application
– file an appeal to Examiner's supervisors, and higher authorities.

There are several other grounds on which a patent application may be rejected by the Examiner. One of them is on the basis of the "Unity of Invention". Sometimes, it may happen that there are claims related to more than one inventive aspect, which by statutory terms means that there is more than one invention contained within one patent application. The Examiner will then request the applicant to divide the application into more than one application. The resulting patent applications are referred to as Divisional Applications. Each of those applications will be treated as a new patent application, and will require the entire set of paper work associated with filing a new patent application, and the fees also. But the priority date of all the divisional applications will be the same as the original date of filing or any priority claimed originally.

Once a patent application has been rejected by the Examiner and the Applicant still doesn't accept the Examiner's position, the Applicant still has the opportunity to be heard by higher authorities. The hierarchy of appealing any decisions in India is as follows: Examiner, Controller, Intellectual Property Appellate Board, High Court and Supreme Court. The first authority immediately above the Examiner would be the Controller General of Patents. If the decision of the Controller is still unsatisfactory to the Applicant, then the decision can be appealed in front of the Intellectual Property Appellate

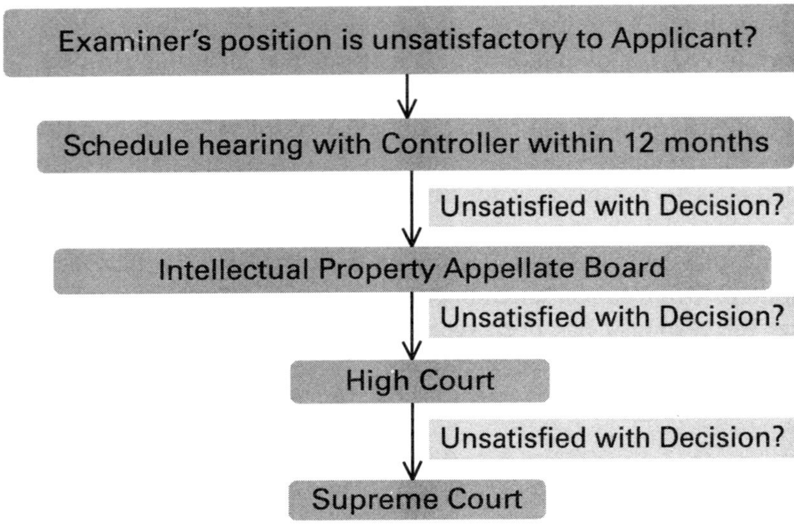

Figure 6. Steps available to the Applicant in case of grievances towards the decisions.

Board (IPAB). Subsequently, any grievances can be taken up with the High Court, followed by the Supreme Court. This is depicted in a flow chart form in Figure 6.

After a patent is granted, as mentioned earlier in the Chapter "Introduction to Patents", maintenance fees have to be paid, the timing for which is given in Table 1.

PATENT PROSECUTION HIGHWAY

There is a new provision by several patent offices across the world with a strong desire to improve the quality of examination of patent applications, and also to improve the turnaround times for disposing patent applications. To this end, what is called a Patent Prosecution Highway PPH has been initiated between several patent offices, wherein if a patent application has been filed in two participating patent office, and if the office of first filing rules that at least one claim in an application is patentable, an applicant may request that the office of second filing fast track the examination of corresponding claims in corresponding applications. The patent offices involved in this patent prosecution highway are given in Table 10.

It can be seen that the filing of the patent application is no end by any means, but only one step in the long chain of events that began with the bright brilliant idea. The examination process takes a while, and for an

Table 10 Patent offices involved in Patent Prosecution Highway

First Patent Office[1]	Second Patent Office[1]	Comments
CIPO	USPTO	A one-year pilot programme commenced on January 28, 2008 and has been extended for a period of two years ending on January 28, 2011, "[in] order to adequately assess the feasibility of the PPH pilot programme".
DKPTO	JPO	Implemented since 1 July 2008.
DKPTO	USPTO	A trial period started on 3 November 2008 and is set to expire 3 November 2009.
EPO	USPTO	A one-year trial cooperation programme ("PPH Pilot Programme") will commence on 29 September 2008, for a period of one year ending on 29 September 2009.
IPAU	USPTO	A one-year pilot programme commenced on April 14, 2008.
JPO	USPTO	The programme has been implemented on a full-time basis since January 4, 2008 after an initial pilot programme that lasted 3 years.
JPO	KIPO	The pilot programme started in April 2007.
JPO	UK-IPO	A one-year pilot programme commenced on July 1, 2007.
JPO	GPTO	A pilot programme will be implemented in March 2008.
JPO	PRH	The pilot will begin on 20 April 2009 and will initially run for two years (until the end of March 2011).
KIPO	USPTO	The Patent Prosecution Highway was implemented on a full-time basis since January 29, 2009 after a one year pilot program.
UK-IPO	USPTO	A one-year pilot program commenced on September 4, 2007and has been extended until further notice.

[1]CIPO: Canadian Intellectual Property Office
EPO: European Patent Office
DEPTO: German Patent and Trademark Office
JPO: Japan Patent Office
KIPO: Korean Intellectual Property Office
UK-IPO: UK Intellectual Property Office
USPTO: United States Patent and Trademark Office
IPAU: IP Australia
DKPTO: Danish Patent and Trademark Office
PRH: National Board of Patents and Registration of Finland

Examiner to actually pick up an application to examine might take anywhere from 2–5 years depending on the technical area involved. Subsequently, the entire communication process between the Examiner and the applicant may take another finite time period, which then culminates in the grant or abandonment of the application. Once the patent has been granted, then it is an enforceable weapon, which can become a powerful tool in the right person's hands, as long as the person knows how to use it.

17

Search and Analysis of Patent Literature

In a WIPO study conducted in 2005, it was reported that an estimated 8,00,000 patents are published worldwide annually. Further, the report states that about 70% of the technical data available in patent literature is not available in any other form, such as technical bulletins, publications, conference proceedings etc. Thus, for maximizing commercial success of any technology-based venture, a strong patent literature analysis must be conducted. Failure to have a comprehensive analysis may result in lack of market exclusivity, inadvertent infringement leading to heavy damages, and loss of revenue, among other things.

Searches may be conducted with various views, depending on the final outcome that is expected. Several types of analyses can be performed once the search has been conducted. But all of them begin with a good search, and the results obtained therefrom. A good search starts with a sound search strategy, and is generally iterative, preferably with different databases that complement each other.

DATABASES

Patent databases are databases that comprise exclusively patent based data. The most significant difference between any other database such as a scientific literature database, and a patent database is that patent database is completely NON-SPECIFIC to any particular technology area. This is in direct contrast to a scientific database which is generally specific to a technology area, such as chemistry, medicine, electronics & electrical engineering, etc. So, a patent database does not differentiate between a patented concept being used in a medical instrument or an aircraft engine. But a particular technology database will show results only from the relevant technical area.

Also, patent database search will show results only from technical fields, as opposed to a regular web search wherein the results are from any source. It is much easier to pick out relevant references from a patent database search as compared to a web search. Further, results from a web search may show results in the list which may not be accessible due to various reasons, such as the page expired, or the page is held under controlled access. A patent database search will at least show the most relevant information such as the bibliographic information. Bibliographic information includes information such as Name of the Inventor(s), Applicant or the Assignee, Title of the Invention, Date of Filing, Date of Grant (if applicable), Abstract, and Drawing. All such information is available from the first page of a patent application or a granted patent, as we have already seen in the Chapter 13 on page 93 'Patent Contents'.

Depending on the source, the database may be limited to a particular jurisdiction or a set of jurisdictions. Further, patent databases may also be limited in terms of the date from which the data is made available.

Individual patent offices provide search abilities, and each differ in their scope and their capabilities that they can offer to the searcher. For example, U.S. Patent & Trademark Office (USPTO) offers online searching of granted patents and published patent applications from the site http://patft.uspto.gov/. This site offers searching ONLY granted U.S. patents and published U.S. patent applications.

European patent databases are all consolidated under one online portal that can be accessed from the website http://ep.espacenet.com/. Each member country of the EP has uploaded its patent information onto this site, and thus, is accessible to anyone who is interested in searching. Further, this site also has data from other sources as well, that includes U.S., Japan, WIPO, Korea, China, India, etc. In all, about 86 jurisdictions' patent related information is available on this site. However, the extent of information is somewhat limited for most of the countries. For some countries such as U.S., and sources such as WIPO, complete patent related information upto a certain time point is available, whereas for most other countries, only bibliographic information is available. Also, the rate of updation from each of the countries varies significantly, and must be checked to know the latest information available.

Similarly, Singapore patent office has data from several patent offices made available through their website http://www.surfip.gov.sg/. The patent jurisdictions whose patent related information can be accessed through this site are: U.S., EP, WIPO, China, Thailand, Singapore, Canada, Taipei, South Korea and U.K. But as we will see later, the fields that can be searched vary for each jurisdiction.

Paid databases for searching include, Delphion®, Micropatent®, Derwent World Patent Index, SciFinder®, CAS, GENESEQ etc. Some of the databases are very specific for particular technology area. For example, SciFinder® is used specifically for chemical structure searching. Similarly, GENESEQ is used for biotechnology related searching for sequences, like gene sequences, nucleotide sequences, protein sequences, and so on. Most of the paid patent databases have patent related information available from a broad jurisdiction coverage.

Depending on the subscription and the fee paid, the information obtained from such paid databases may be quite up-to-date and recent. Other databases may have a lead time before the information is made available. Some databases process the information made available from the patent offices and make it more readable, by giving it their own abstract and title, thereby increasing the relevancy of a search. However, in such instances, a lead time exists to accommodate the time required to process the patent office data.

Other good resources for searching also include www.ip.com, http://www.freepatentsonline.com/ (which also, incidentally has a chemical structure searching facility built within), Google® patents, Google® itself, and so on. Caution must be exercised while accessing these freely available databases, for the information updation, and the availability may not be regular and not very timely.

SEARCH STRATEGY

A search strategy is a compilation of words that is generally synonymous with the concept(s) that is being searched for, and the field(s) to be searched. The words to be searched, generally termed keywords, need to be carefully chosen so as not to miss any relevant reference. Keywords have to be chosen appropriately so as to encompass every possible representation of the concept being sought after. For example, when one is searching for 'machines', then the main concept to be searched for is 'machine'. Immediately, a whole set of synonyms need to be drawn up, and that may include, 'motor', 'engine', etc. As many synonyms as possible need to be arrived at, and used to draw up the search strategy.

Once the concept and the corresponding synonyms are obtained, then they must be connected with appropriate operators. These operators are the same as Boolean operators. The Boolean operators functions in exactly the same manner here as they do in a mathematical sense. The operators include AND, OR, and NOT. If two keywords are connected by an AND operator, then both keywords have to be present in one reference for that reference to be shown as a result hit. For example, if the search strategy is 'machine AND operator', then both the words machine and operator have to be present in the same reference so as to render the reference as part of the result hit. Similarly, this logic can be extended to more than two keywords. One example is 'machine AND operator AND signal AND radar', wherein all of the keywords mentioned have to be present in one reference for that reference to become part of a result hit.

On the other hand, an OR operator acts in such a way that if two keywords are connected by it, then if any one of the keywords is present in the reference, then that reference becomes part of the results hit. Thus, in a search strategy 'machine OR engine' if either one of these words are present in the reference, that reference becomes part of the results hit. This concept can be extended to any number of keywords to be used. An example would be 'engine OR machine OR apparatus OR equipment' will return all the references that contain any one of those keywords. It should also be noted that those references that contain more than one of the keywords will also be part of the results set.

NOT is an operator which when used with a keyword, the search engine looks for all the references that does NOT contain that particular keyword. For example, a search strategy 'machine NOT engine' will return all documents that have the keyword machine and DO NOT contain engine. Sometimes this operator is used as ANDNOT instead of simply NOT.

Further, there are wildcard operators or wildcards available to the searcher. These wildcards are used to substitute any unknown character. Depending on the database and the wildcard used, the wildcards may represent only one character or it may represent more than one character. Wildcards are generally represented by the asterisk symbol '*', or by a question mark '?'. In many databases, a * is a wildcard used to represent many characters, and a ? is a wildcard used for only one character. The symbol '*' is typically used in the following manner: 'wipe*', which means every patent that has 'wipe', 'wipes', 'wiped', 'wiper' etc. will be picked up. Similarly, T??TH will pick up TOOTH, TEETH, TRUTH, etc., basically any word that has two alphabets between T and TH.

Another operator frequently found useful is the ADJ or NEAR operator. Once again, the database used will determine which of these two are the most relevant operators. In some databases, both these operators are in use, with the assigned meaning to each and their appropriate use being different. These operators are used to join two keywords to indicate that the two keywords are within each other's proximity. Thus, the search strategy 'machine ADJ operator' will return only those references where the words 'machine' and 'operator' are within a one-word distance of each other. Again, depending on the database used, the order may also be important. If the order is important, then the search strategy must take that into account. The ADJ or NEAR operators may also be present with a numeral at the end. The numeral will indicate the distance between the two keywords in use. Thus, as an illustration, the search strategy ‘machine ADJ3 operator’ will return references containing ‘machine operator’ and those that contain phrases like ‘machine or engine operator’, and sometimes even ‘operator of a machine’.

Keyword searches are the easiest to perform, and perhaps most powerful even. This is due to the fact that all other forms of information like a drawing or a chemical structure are not very conducive for searching. Keywords are part of a text that can be easily made into a searchable form, and consequently, easily searched. The challenge for a searcher is to be able to come up with a proper search strategy that gives very relevant results set, and not be inundated with a lot of “noise”.

In most practical situations, the searcher is presented with an idea for an invention for which a proper relevant reference list has to be generated for appropriate review. This involves first understanding the invention – usually given in free style English language. Once a thorough understanding of the invention is established, then this has to be converted into a search strategy. This requires understanding the concept being asked for by the requester and appropriately developing a strong search strategy. For instance, someone might ask for ‘perfumes associated with wipes’. This needs to be broken into concepts for searching. One search concept would be ‘wipes’, synonyms for which may be ‘tissues’, and so on. Synonyms may also be phrases such ‘paper napkins’. Then the next concept would be ‘perfumes’. Other synonyms for it could be ‘scents’. Subsequently, all the concepts, including the synonyms have to be put together in an appropriate manner to form the search strategy. All the synonyms for each concept are combined with the operator ‘OR’. Each of these concepts need to be combined with an ‘AND’. Thus, the search strategy for this would be ((‘wipes’ OR ‘tissues’) AND (‘perfumes’ OR ‘scents’)).

An easy way to do the same would be to construct a table giving the concepts and synonyms in Table 11.

Table 11 An illustration of the search strategy arrived at by following the steps.

	Concepts		
	C_1	C_2	C_3
	$S_{1,1}$	$S_{2,1}$	$S_{3,1}$
Synonyms	$S_{1,2}$	$S_{2,2}$	$S_{3,2}$
	$S_{1,3}$	$S_{2,3}$	$S_{3,3}$
	$S_{1,4}$	$S_{2,4}$	$S_{3,4}$

Once this table has been generated, it is becomes very simple to construct the search strategy, which in this case would be (($S_{1,1}$ OR $S_{1,2}$ OR $S_{1,3}$ OR $S_{1,4}$) AND ($S_{2,1}$ OR $S_{2,2}$ OR $S_{2,3}$ OR $S_{2,4}$) AND ($S_{3,1}$ OR $S_{3,2}$ OR $S_{3,3}$ OR $S_{3,4}$)). Of course, it must be understood that there is no necessity each and every concept will result in the same number of synonyms. So, whereas one concept will end up having 7 synonyms, the other may have only 3.

The other important point about generating a table of this nature is that at any point in the future, the search strategy can be easily traced, and any mistakes and/or oversights can be picked up by simply viewing the table quickly.

The search strategy for the above-mentioned example would be something along the lines of '((perfume* OR scent*) AND (wipe OR tissue OR paper OR napkin))'. Once the search strategy has been used to search in a particular database, the results set need to be scanned to check to see if there are any other synonyms that were used for the concepts. If any were found, then this word also needs to be included in the search strategy, and the search then has to be run again to capture any references that may have been missed. This has to be repeated as many times as it takes to obtain redundant results.

Patent literature is also notorious for representing words and concepts in a different manner than what is generally spoken or written. For instance, the concept 'wipes' may also be represented as 'wiping aid'. This is done for various reasons, some of which include to obtain broader coverage, or to avoid detection by searches so as to catch potential infringers flat-footed. Thus, an efficient searcher needs to be aware of various ways of representing the same concept, the more number of ways that can be envisioned, the stronger the search strategy. Another key feature of a good search strategy is the ability to capture many concepts with fewer keywords. Thus, to capture 'wipe', 'wipes', 'wiping', and ' wiped', one keyword 'wip*' can be used effectively. However, the searcher must also be aware of any potential noise that can arise from such search strategies. In this instance, 'wip*' will also pick up patents containing 'wipo'.

FIELDS OF SEARCH

The other aspect of searching, besides the search strategy, involves the field of search. Databases provide the option of searching for the following fields specifically: Claims; Title; Abstract; Claims, Title & Abstract; Description; Inventor(s); Assignee; Patent/Publication Number; and so on. Some other search databases such as the one on USPTO website provides the option of even searching for attorneys. Each database has some capability, and allows for searching different fields. The database help section has to consulted to find out which of the fields searching is supported by the database. The choice of field depends on the nature of the analysis to be conducted.

Searches may also be conducted in more than one field for more than one concept. For example, a keyword can be searched for in the 'Claims' and then the search results can be narrowed down using 'Inventors'. Searches can also be narrowed down using Classification Codes. (See Classification Codes, under Front Page in Chapter 13 on page 93 Patent Contents). Classification codes can be used effectively to narrow down search results from a keyword to one particular technical area, thus making it easier to zoom in on only the most relevant patents.

Searches can also be limited to particular date ranges, countries, languages and so on. These kinds of restrictions may be required for various reasons (See section on Analyses). The format of the date varies with the database in question, and the appropriate database's help section must be consulted before keying in that field.

While conducting searches, it is very useful to have a seed reference on hand. A seed reference is a reference that you already know is relevant to the subject you are searching. As a searcher, there are several ways of becoming aware of a seed reference. The requester, such as the inventor or an attorney may provide the seed reference. Alternately, a quick rough search in a web search engine may be done to pick up a reference that is most relevant. A seed reference is useful in that when the search itself is conducted, the presence of the seed reference will validate the search strategy to be relevant. Further, the seed reference also helps in coming up with keywords useful for the searches.

A flow chart for arriving at a search strategy is given in Figure 7.

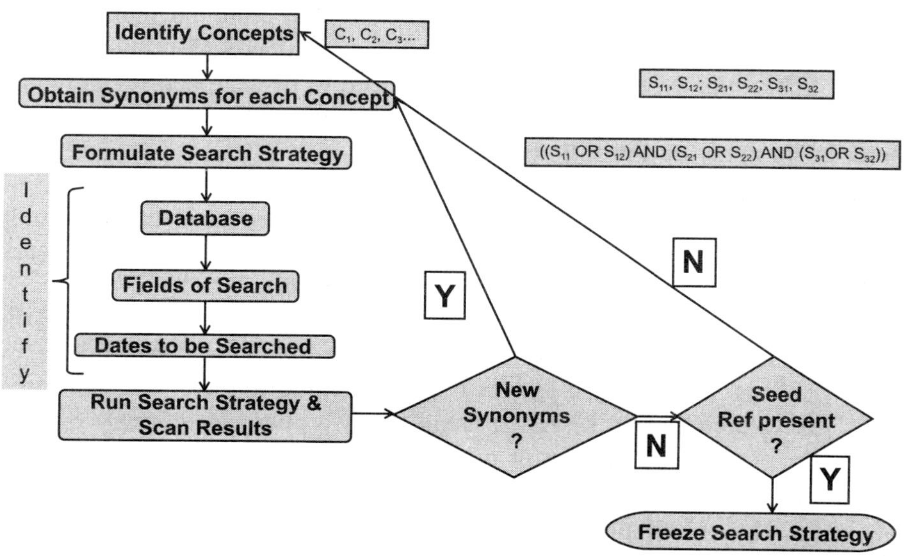

Figure 7. Flow chart to arrive at a finalized Search Strategy.

PATENT ANALYSES

Analysis of search results requires patience and diligence to do a thorough job and to do justice to the search results and the requester. To perform analysis, it is useful to understand the nature of analysis requested. Once the technical features of the request has been understood, a good search strategy can be assimilated based on concepts and synonyms. Subsequently, the proper fields of search have to be chosen. For this to be done properly, the nature of the analysis has to be clearly understood. The types of patent literature analysis are:

- Freedom-to-Operate
- Infringement
- Invalidation or Opposition
- Patentability
- Landscape

Each of these types of analysis has a certain nuance associated with it, and has to be taken into account while conducting the search itself, and subsequently, in the analysis of the reference.

Freedom-to-Operate (FTO), also called 'Freedom-to-Practice (FTP)' or 'Clearance', or 'Non-Infringement' analysis is necessary to ascertain a product being sold or intended to be sold in a market does not infringe on any existing enforceable patents. A search that is directed towards a FTP analysis needs the following inputs: the countries in which the product is sold/to be sold, the date on which the product is to be launched/was launched, any patents owned by the company that is selling/intending to sell it. Subsequently, the patent databases need to be searched for only patents that are active in those particular jurisdictions. That is, the search can be done by applying the following conditions:

(i) dates for which the patents are to be searched need to range only from the date of launch to 20 years prior to the date of launch, hence the date fields should be appropriately chosen;
(ii) the countries to be searched should be restricted to those where the products are to be sold/intended to be sold. This can be done by looking at only those patents that are granted in the country of interest, which can be searched using the two character country code in the publication number or patent number field;
(iii) the features of the products being sold/to be sold have to be CLAIMED in the patents. So, the search strategy from the concepts or features can be restricted to only the 'Claims' section of the patent;

(iv) any relevant patents identified must be checked continuously for the maintenance fee status. This is because the patents need to be maintained to be enforced. Thus, if the maintenance fee has not been paid, then patent can be assumed to have lapsed. But care must be taken before arriving at this conclusion, for even if the maintenance fee is not paid, a fine or surcharge may be paid to reinstate the patent. So sufficient time must be given before deeming a patent unenforceable. Maintenance fee payment data may be found at the relevant patent office, either through electronic means, or upon request.

Another aspect that can be taken into account while conducting this analysis is to exclude all patents that are owned by the requesters themselves, because products that contain features claimed in their own patents do not necessarily constitute an act of infringement. Figure 8 gives a flowchart for the process involved in a Freedom-To-Operate Analysis.

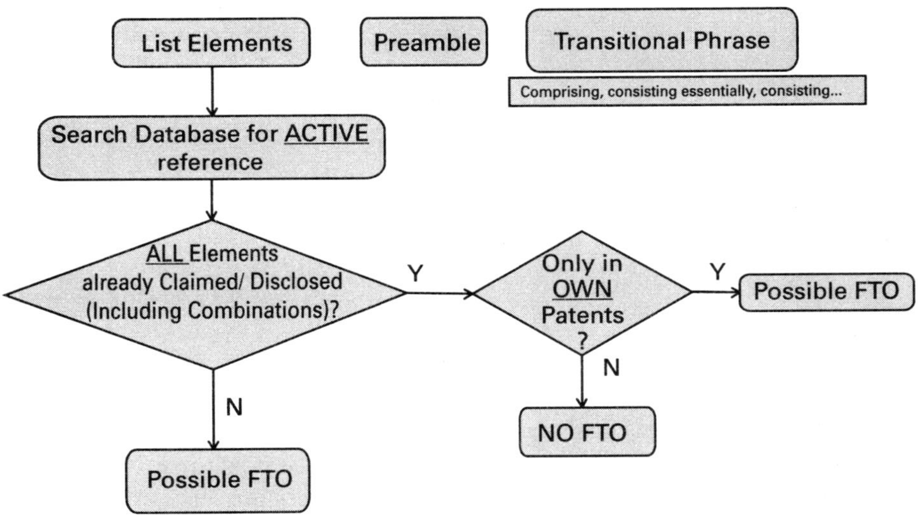

Figure 8. Flowchart for the process involved in a Freedom-To-Operate Analysis.

Infringement is said to occur when whoever without authority makes, uses, or sells any invention patented by another in the jurisdiction. An infringement analysis is hence done to determine if a product being made, used or sold infringes on the claims of a patent. Thus, an infringement analysis involves similar search and analysis procedure as that of an FTO analysis. In this instance, the features or components of the product in question are listed in detail, and subsequently, the patent literature needs to be searched if a feature or component or combinations of features or components are CLAIMED in any active and enforceable patent. Searching can be limited to the effective period, which would typically be 20 years prior to the date of making, using or selling of the product, and the field to be searched may be limited to the claims.

An infringement analysis is, in effect, the reverse of a FTO analysis. Hence, for this reason, FTO analysis is also sometimes referred to as a Non-Infringement analysis. Figure 9 gives a flowchart for the process involved in an Infringement Analysis.

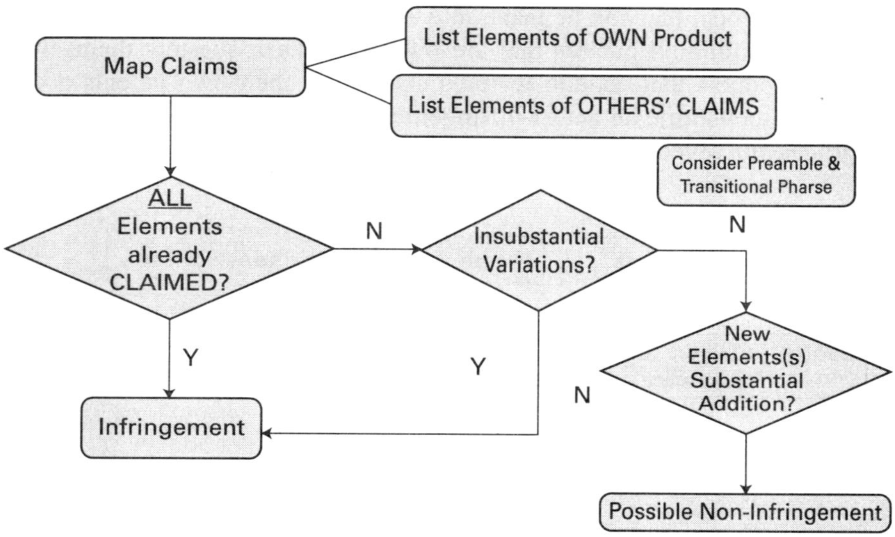

Figure 9. Flowchart for the process involved in an Infringement Analysis.

Invalidation analysis is done to render claims of patents unenforceable. Invalidation, as used herein, depending on the context, may sometimes also encompass **Opposition**. In opposition proceedings, concerned patent office is involved in resolving the issues related to validity of the patent document. In Invalidation proceeding, the concerned parties may decide to resolve the differences between themselves. Alternately, one party may decide to take a judiciary course to challenge the validity of the patent. Also, opposition proceedings must be done within a certain time period. Two different kinds of Opposition proceedings are present, depending on when the proceedings are begun. Opposition proceeding started any time before the grant of a patent is referred to as Pre-Grant Opposition, while Opposition proceeding started any time upto a certain time period after the grant of a patent is referred to as Post-Grant Opposition. The Opposition proceedings are initiated with the patent office.

In India, the post-grant opposition can be made upto one year after the grant of a patent. In Europe, post-grant opposition can be initiated within 9 months after grant of a patent. In U.S., opposition proceedings can be initiated at any time after the grant of a patent. After the expiry of the appropriate time periods, only judicial proceedings can be initiated to challenge the validity of a patent. Further, if the decision of the patent office is not satisfactory to any of the parties, then the aggrieved party can challenge the decision on a higher court through a judicial proceedings.

The most common way of invalidation is to provide references that disclose the claimed invention prior to the date of priority, preferably, at least one year prior to the date of priority. This one year gap is taken to negate any grace periods that may be present in a given jurisdiction. The references cited generally should not be already considered by the examiner(s) before the grant of the patent (although it can be cited as 'not having been considered in this new light').

Typically, specific claims that need to be invalidated are pointed out, and the references relevant to those particular claims are to be provided. Thus, all kinds of references, regardless of patent or not can be cited, as long as they are dated to at least one year prior to the priority date of patent. Thus, searches can be from broad sources such as internet, libraries, any conferences or trade show bulletins etc. Dates to be searched should be anything earlier than the priority date, so the date fields in the databases should be appropriately chosen.

Other grounds for invalidation also exist. The reasons for invalidation may be varied and are typically jurisdiction dependent. The laws of the corresponding jurisdiction should be consulted to ascertain all the grounds for opposition, or invalidation. The procedure for opposition/ invalidation must also be consulted, and the appropriate steps need to be taken. Most often, any reason can be used to raise objections against the grant of a patent. These may include reasons, such as, wrong inventorship, not bringing a known reference to light, too broad scope claimed, insufficient enablement, subject matter being frivolous, subject matter being against *ordre public*, and so on. Also, some jurisdictions specify time periods within which invalidation proceedings need to be started. The specific grounds for opposition of grant of patents in India are given in Section 25, and are as follows: (The sub-sections are, in some places, generally paraphrased).

(a) the applicant for the patent wrongfully obtained the invention;
(b) that the claimed invention has been published before the priority date;
(c) that the claimed invention is already claimed in another complete specification whose priority date was earlier than but was published on or after the priority date of the applicant's claim, as long as the application for a patent in India;

(d) that the claimed invention was publicly known or publicly used in India before the priority date of that claim;
(e) that the claimed invention is obvious and clearly does not involve any inventive step;
(f) that the subject of any claim of the complete specification is not an invention within the meaning of this Act, or is not patentable under this Act;
(g) that the complete specification does not sufficiently and clearly describe the invention or the method by which it is to be performed;
(h) that the applicant has failed to disclose to the Controller the information regarding related foreign applications;
(i) the application was not made within twelve months from the date of the first application in a convention country;
(j) that the complete specification does not disclose or wrongly mentions the source or geographic origin of biological material used for the invention;
(k) that the claimed invention is anticipated having regard to the knowledge, oral or otherwise, available within any local or indigenous community in India or elsewhere.

Figure 10 gives a flowchart for the process involved in an Invalidation Analysis based on prior art.

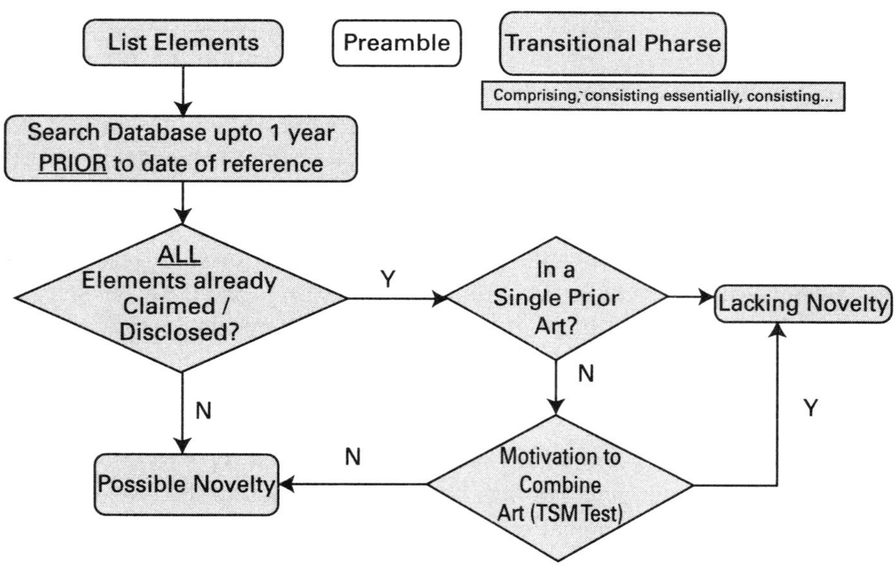

Figure 10. Flowchart for the process involved in an Invalidation Analysis based on prior art.

Patentability analysis is done to determine the patentability of an invention. This type of analysis, in the simplest level, provides an opinion as to whether an invention as envisioned is patentable or not, thus making it very black-and-white. But in fact, the analysis can provide greater insights into the patentability of an invention as envisioned by providing more data, such as providing the scope of all other disclosed material in the literature in relation to the invention as envisioned. This information will provide better ideas as to whether the scope of invention needs to be narrowed down, or can be expanded (provided there is sufficient data to support it).

A facile way to conduct a patentability analysis is to list all the novel features of the invention as presented and mapping them against any already published references for each respective novel feature. To achieve this, a patentability analysis has to encompass results of search conducted in all the available databases, including non-patent literature and even internet search engine results, for any kind of disclosure of the invention as envisioned. The search also should not be limited to any dates, and must continue till the date of filing of the patent application. For filing in U.S., as noted earlier, all the references material to the patentability should be brought to the notice of the patent office. (See Chapter 15 on page 113 Filing Patent Applications). Figure 11 gives a flowchart for the process involved in a Patentability Analysis.

Landscape analyses, or Landscapes, as they are referred to in regular parlance, are done to provide a snapshot at the trends or developments in a certain area. A landscape workproduct gives an idea, typically one-page graphical representation, of trends. Trends may be quite varied, some

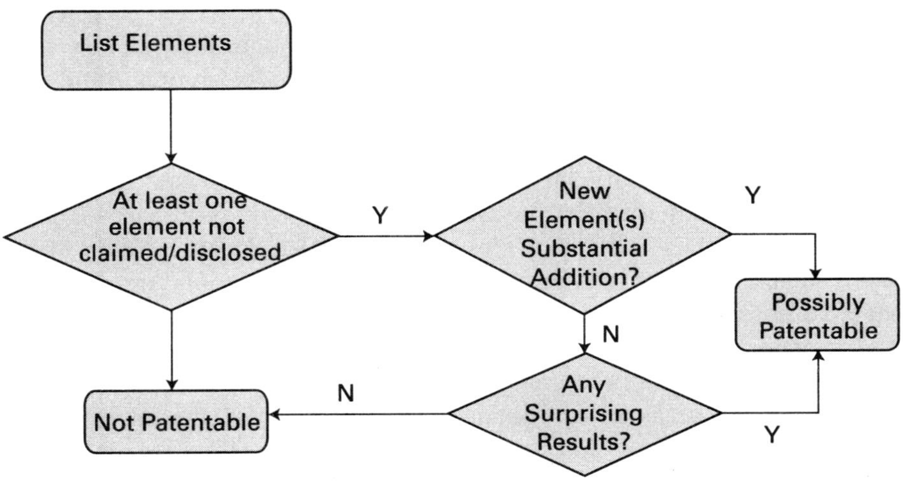

Figure 11. Flowchart for the process involved in a Patentability Analysis.

examples of which include: the use of a certain material over the years, emerging trends in the field, a competitors patenting trend (and hence possible strategy), and so on. The search may not necessarily be limited to patent literature, but as mentioned earlier, since patent literature contains more technical information than anywhere else, it is a great place to conduct searches.

A search geared towards landscape analyses is dependent on the nature of landscape requested. Thus, for a 'competitor watch' in a particular field, besides the keywords representing the field, the search can be narrowed down by the use of competitor's name as the assignee. Care must be taken to ensure that all references are captured because some patents may not be assigned directly to the competitor, this is especially true for patent application publications. Identifying and including names of inventors associated with the assignee in question and the field may be advantageous. Further to complicate matters, the name of a competitor may be represented variously in different patents. For example, a thorough search for patents by GE must also include names like General Electric, General Electric Co., General Electric Company etc.

A frequent inference that is desired from landscapes is one of a predictive kind. Thus, in a competitor watch, the competitor's next step can be guessed at. Similarly, in a trend analysis, prediction of the most probable next trend will be desired. This is done for several reasons, one of which may include an educated decision in taking the next step (usually by senior management).

Another very commonly requested inference from landscapes is what is called a 'Gap Analysis', also known as 'White Space Analysis'. This kind of analysis studies the trends in a particular field and identifies gaps that have not been explored. Typically, this requires some technical expertise to understand what the gaps are, and many times, there may be a good reason for the existence of the gap. In some instances though, the gap may have occurred due to oversight or other reasons, but provides an opportunity for one to exploit for one's own benefit. Providing insights into the existence of such gaps will be of paramount importance to one in that field.

Some other proprietary tools are available at the analysts' disposal to visualize the patent literature in a facile manner. One particular example is the Aureka® map which provides a colour coded "contour" map of the patent landscape in a relevant technology area. Such tools are generally available on a subscription basis, and sometimes may prove expensive to use/maintain. Such tools may also be internally developed and customized to suit an organization's requirement.

Whatever the reasons for conducting the search and the analyses, the results set may comprise too many references. Whether the results set has too many references or not, depends on the time available for the analysis. If the time available is less, then the next step to be undertaken to narrow down the search is to screen the titles of the references. Once this is done, the abstract and the drawings may be used for the next level of screening. Subsequently, the claims and the description have to be studied carefully to qualify the reference as relevant or not.

SEARCH REPORTS

Once a search has been conducted, and an analysis of the search results as thoroughly as the job demanded performed, providing a report of the analysis results is generally required. The search report must contain all the salient points that require highlighting, and some manner of providing details as well, wherever necessary. A graphical representation is usually quite appealing, but must be supplemented with text to provide the desired impact.

A complete search & analyses report must contain information such as the database used for searching, dates searched, search strategy, the fields searched, and an appropriate disclaimer. The disclaimer stated is an Explicit Disclaimer. Another kind of disclaimer is the Implicit Disclaimer, which is not explicitly stated but implicitly hinted at. Such disclaimers can be arrived at from the use of dates of searching, which automatically states that any reference outside that date range does not fall under this search. Similarly, the mention of a database used for searching is also an implicit disclaimer, as different databases are updated at varying time periods, thus depending on when the search was conducted, some references may not be picked up at all. It must be emphasized that the searcher must be fully aware of the limitations of the databases used.

Wherever and whenever necessary, embedding the actual files that provide more details is also useful, and recommended. It should be noted that embedding increases the file size, and oftentimes cannot be sent over email, but this limitation may be overcome by uploading the file onto a secure website accessible to restricted personnel.

On many occasions, explicit statements such as "This is easily patentable" or "This reference is sitting right on top of the invention" are not preferred by some requesters, for several very good reasons. Softer and subtler suggestions are desirable, such as "Reference Number: ___ Line Numbers ___ to ___ states that..." Providing a visual diagram mapping the different elements or aspects between two or more different references is a good way of depicting the information. It has been found that such depictions quickly transfer the information with very less ambiguity. Subtle emphasis can be used, such as colour variations, bolding, highlighting, etc.

A good searcher must understand the request first and foremost. This is not only related to understanding the technical features associated with the request, but also to the nature of the final analysis – patentability, FTP, opposition etc. This second aspect is a very important side of the analysis that is often overlooked. Once this is well understood, then a good search strategy can be expected. A good search strategy will result in high relevance results set. Subsequently, the analysis of the reference will become easier with high relevance results set. It is a long chain that is well interlinked and each link cannot be ignored or considered any less important than the other.

18

Case Laws and Their Significance

ARVIND VISWANATHAN
Xellect IP Solutions, Bangalore
&
MALATHI LAKSHMIKUMARAN
Lakshmikumaran & Sridharan, Delhi

IPR is a quasi-legal subject, in that it is built within a legal framework to provide protection for matters that may be technical, artistic or combinations. Hence, it is important to have a reasonable understanding about the nature of the legal systems in place, and how the systems will use the law towards a particular case.

Legal systems can be broadly classified into two different kinds: Common law system, and Civil Law System. Most of the legal systems evolved from either one or the other, and are still predominantly common law or civil law. However, a mix of both in a legal systems is also present.

A Common Law system is a legal system that is developed through the decisions of courts and similar tribunals. The law is generally created and refined by judges. Interpretations of the laws and the rules and guidelines for following the law are also laid down by the judges, and judgements in cases. Whenever there is no authoritative statement of the law, the judges have the authority, and indeed the duty to make the law and create precedents. The effect of this legal system is that any subsequent judgements for a case are bound by judgement of any preceding similar cases. Hence, judges have to be very careful and deliberate in pronouncing judgements for a case. India follows a predominantly a common law system.

On the other hand, in a Civil Law system, local compilations of legal principles are recognized as normative and legislations are the primary source of law. Courts, and judges, use the provisions of codes and statutes as the primary source for providing judgements. Preceding cases and past judgements are used only as guidelines.

Thus, in a case where there is not enough clarity as to the nature of judgement that may be pronounced, case laws provide a very good guideline as to the fate of the case at hand. Case laws also serve as an important source of information about trends in patenting laws. With respect to any patent applications that is being examined in a patent office, or a judgment by an Examiner is being appealed in a court, the nature of the judgment and the fate of the case regarding patentability in a particular field of technology can be resolved based on prevailing case law.

India is still maturing in terms of patent cases having been fought in courts, and establishing precedents. More mature patenting systems such as U.S. and Europe have many more cases that have established very good precedents. India has taken advantage of the precedents set in these advanced systems in setting up the laws for patenting, during the later rounds of amendments, especially in terms of biotechnology and software patenting, among other things.

Here, a case law digest from U.S. and Europe is given to provide an idea as to how the patenting systems evolved from their early days, to its present system. It must be borne in mind that this system is still evolving and maturing as the days progress. This is but a handful of cases to give an idea. There are many more cases that have helped the system mature and evolve over time. We have not attempted to provide a compendium here, but a mere snapshot of cases.

The case laws are divided into the four main criteria for obtaining a patent viz. Patentable Subject Matter, Novelty, Non-Obviousness or Inventive Step and Utility or Industrial Applicability.

I. PATENTABLE SUBJECT-MATTER

I.1 USA—General Exceptions, Software, Business Methods:

1. O'Reilly v. Morse, 56 U.S. (15 How.) 62 (1853): Morse was allowed a patent for a process of using electromagnetism to produce distinguishable signs for telegraphy. His eighth claim read:

"I do not propose to limit myself to the specific machinery or parts of machinery described in the foregoing specification and claims;

the essence of my invention being the use of the motive power of the electric or galvanic current, which I call electro-magnetism, however developed for marking or printing intelligible characters, signs, or letters, at any distances, being a new application of that power of which I claim to be the first inventor or discoverer."

The court considered the italicized portion and held it to be too broad and not patentable. In the opinion of the court, the claim extended to monopolizing electro-magnetism to communicate. The court held that he was claiming over the principle or the abstract theory that galvanic current could be used to print letters and signs, which would not be permitted. But the claim over his structure to make use of this principle was held to be patentable subject-matter.

2. Parker v. Flook, 437 U.S. 584 (1978): Flook applied for a patent on "Methods of Updating Alarm Limits" to be employed in catalytic conversion processes, wherein the alarm limit to indicate inefficiency or danger was to be updated according to the operating conditions of the process. The claim was on the method of updating in itself, which consisted of three steps:

   - Measure the existing value of a variable like temperature, pressure etc.;
   - Apply an algorithm to calculate an updated alarm limit value based on these updated values;
   - Adjusting the actual alarm limit to the updated value.

The novelty rested in the algorithm. Re-iterating *O'Reilly v. Morse*, the court held that a novel and useful structure created with the help of a principle is patentable, a scientific truth or principle, or a mathematical algorithm or formula, and a natural phenomenon or laws of nature, are not patentable *per se*.

3. Diamond v. Diehr, 450 U.S. 175 (1981): The claimed invention was a process for molding raw, uncured synthetic rubber into cured precision products, several of the steps using a mathematical formula. Perfect curing is a function of thickness, temperature and time, which continuously varied throughout the process and the invention used to feed this data continuously into a programmed digital computer to calculate the timing to remove the product from the process. This calculation was based on the famous Arrhenius equation.

The court held that an invention which implements or uses a mathematical formula is different from an invention which claims the formula in the abstract. Unlike prior cases where the applicant's patent would have preempted a natural phenomenon, scientific principle or mathematical formula, the present claim was only over the process as a whole, which did not have the same effect. And process patents being allowed under law, it does not lose its patentability merely because it employs a formula in one of its steps.

4. In re: Alappat, 33 F.3d 1536 (Fed. Cir. 1994) (en banc): The invention employed an anti-aliasing technique to remove distortions in visually represented waveform. Alappat's claims are drawn to a so-called 'rasterizer' which is used in a digital oscilloscope to smooth waveform data prior to displaying the waveform on the oscilloscope screen. The invention lies in the general architecture and operation of the rasterizer to substantially eliminate the appearance of discontinuities in the waveform by changing the intensity of each pixel depending on the pixel's proximity to a waveform vector.

The court employed the "claims as a whole" approach stated in the cases of *Parker v. Flook & Diamond v. Diehr* and held that a programmed general purpose computer becomes a new machine once a computer program is loaded into memory, and is therefore eligible for patent protection as a machine. Therefore, although the invention involved a computer program, the claim was directed to the machine and not the program *per se*. Once the program is loaded, it gives rise to new qualities and properties and causes the computer to function in a manner different from normal computers.

5. In Re Lowry, 32 F.3d 1579 (Fed. Cir. 1994): The patent in this case was a "Data Processing System Having a Data Structure with a Single, Simple Primitive" and the claim was directed towards a memory storing data in a particular data structure, which was organized in a particular manner for efficient functioning. The data was stored according to a particular order or arrangement. The order or arrangement to be followed in storing the data was defined by a Data Model. Therefore, data structures are the physical implementation of a data model's organization of the data. Application programs use this stored data to perform specified functions.

In rejecting the printed matter doctrine in this case, the court held that the matter was anyway not directed to a human mind; instead the information was being processed by a machine. Secondly, the court held that the data structure were functionally and structurally related to the memory, in the sense that management of information for computing efficiency, in hardware terms, meant physical organization on the information stored in memory in the form of specific electrical or magnetic structural elements in a memory.

Therefore, the invention was held not to be excluded from patentability.

6. State Street Bank & Trust Co. v. Signature Financial Group, 149 F.3d 1368 (Fed. Cir. 1998): At issue in this case was a patent titled "Data Processing System for Hub and Spoke Financial Services Configuration". Essentially the data processing system facilitated a structure wherein mutual funds pool their assets into an investment portfolio organized as a partnership. The PTO as rejected the claim on grounds that the patentee is trying to claim a business method and that the processing system employs algorithms formulas and thus not patentable.

In rejecting these arguments, the court held that the transformation of data, representing discrete dollar amounts, through a series of mathematical calculations, by a machine, into a final share price, constitutes a practical application of a mathematical algorithm, formula or calculation because it produces a useful, concrete, and tangible result. The final share price is momentarily fixed for recording and reporting purposes and is even accepted and relied upon by regulatory authorities and in subsequent trades. With regard to the first objection that it is a business method, the court noted that till date no court had ever invoked this exception and when the invention is directed to a process or a method and producing a useful, concrete, and tangible result, it would not be rejected just because the method was directed towards business since that was not a mandate in the legislation. The court did not want to create a new exception to the broad patentability rule in the USA.

I.2 US—Biological Material, Public Policy:

1. Diamond vs. Chakrabarty, 447 U.S. 303 (1980): The patentee had developed a bacterium (derived from the Pseudomonas genus) capable of breaking down crude oil, which he proposed to use in treating oil spills. His patent application was rejected on the grounds that it was a living thing and therefore a product of nature.

Holding that *anything under the sun that is made by man* is patentable, the Supreme Court opined that "*the fact that micro-organisms are alive is without legal significance for purposes of the patent law.*" What mattered according to the court was whether it was a discovery of a product of nature or it involved human skill and ingenuity. Chakrabarty's bacterium was created in a laboratory through cross breeding and therefore it was held not to be "nature's handiwork," but the product of "human ingenuity and research." On this ground, it was held to be patentable subject-matter.

2. Ex Parte Allen, 2 U.S.P.Q.2d (BNA) 1425 (Bd. Pat. Appeals & Interferences 1987), aff'd, 846 F.2d 77 (Fed. Cir. 1998): While the case of

Diamond vs. Chakrabarty involved a bacterium, this case involved a patent directed towards a multi-cellular animal, a polyploidy oyster. The oyster has been genetically modified to have increased growth and be edible throughout all stages of its life cycle. The PTO took a similar objection that the oyster was not patentable being a living thing and thus a product of nature. On appeal, the Board of Patent Appeals and Interferences set aside the decision and allowed for patentability of the oyster citing *Diamond vs. Chakrabarty*. The Board noted that the test was not whether the subject-matter was controlled by the laws of nature; rather the subject-matter claimed must be occurring in nature. The claimed oyster was created in the laboratory and thus not a product of nature.

I.3 USA—Public Policy/Morality:

1. Lowell v. Lewis, 15 F. Cas. 1018 (C.C.D. Mass. 1817): This case on the patentability of a water pump concerns the "moral utility" of subject matter for the purposes of patenting. In a suit for infringement, the infringer claimed the defense that the patent is invalid for not being useful. The contention was that his pump would be 'useful' only if he can prove that it has better utility than already existing pumps. In rejecting this contention, the court held that the word 'useful' occurring in the legislation in the USA was only meant to prevent the patenting of mischievous or immoral devices. It was held that an invention should not be frivolous or "injurious to the well being, good policy, or sound morals of society" to fulfill the utility requirement.
2. Stuart Newman's 'Humouse' patent application; see USPTO, Facts on Patenting Life Forms Having a Relationship to Humans, April 1 1998, http://uspto.gov/web/offices/com/speeches/98-06.htm: This application sought to patent a technique for combining human and animal embryonic cells to produce a human-mouse embryo, ("Humouse") which could be implanted into a surrogate mother resulting in the development of a being having mixed human and animal composition. This patent was rejected by the PTO holding that they fail to meet the "public policy and morality aspects" of the utility requirement. After this, the PTO expressly stated that any patent or claim directed to or including within its scope a human being would not be patentable.

I.4 Europe—Software/Business Method:

1. In Re Vicom Systems, Inc., 1987 E.P.O.R 74 (Tech. Bd. App. 1986): Vicom Systems, a California-based incorporation, filed an application

for a “Method and apparatus for improved digital image processing”. The application included claims for both a method and an apparatus. The Examining Division held that the method claims were related to a mathematical method and therefore excluded.

The Technical Board of Appeal reversed, noting that digital image processing is not an abstract process but a “real world activity” and held that “even if the idea underlying an invention may be considered to reside in a mathematical method, *a claim directed to a technical process in which the method is used does not seek protection for the mathematical method as such*.” The Board thus wiggled its way out by highlighting on the last two words of the exception to patentability: “as such”. The approach is very similar to the one in USA where the claim as a whole is considered and the claim is not divided into technical and non-technical parts. The Board further held that for such claims to satisfy the invention requirement, it must be directed to a technical art, in the sense that invention has a “technical effect” in improving performance of an apparatus or process; even improving a computer itself would fulfill this requirement. On facts, the court held that the claim satisfied this requirement since it resulted in a much more efficient machine.

2. In Re Pension Benefit Sys. P’ship, 2002 E.P.O.R 522 (Tech. Bd. App. 1999): The EPO rejected a patent application by Pension Benefit Systems Partnership in respect of a method of controlling a pension benefits program. The method that was actually being claimed was nothing but the computerized activities of the real world professional working in that field. The Board of Appeals rejected the claim on the grounds that the method claim did not produce any technical effect.

The Board of Appeal considered the method claim and found that apart from various computing means mentioned in that claim, it was directed to a method for controlling a pension benefits program. Its actual implementation in the computer was never described or claimed whereby some technical element could have been detected. It found all the features of the claim to be “*steps of processing and producing information having purely administrative, actuarial and/or financial character*.” Processing and producing such information were held to be typical steps of business and economic methods. It found the invention as claimed did not go beyond a *method of doing business as such*.

I.5 Europe—Biological Material/Morality & Public Ordre

1. Howard Florey Institute/Relaxin Case (V008/94), 1995 O.J.E.P.O. 545: Here, the claims were toward a method for synthesis of peptides

with relaxin activity, which included synthesis of relaxin and certain analogues of relaxin. Relaxin is an ovarian hormone that softens and lengthens the inter-pubic ligaments during pregnancy. It also dilates the cervix and inhibits contractions of the uterus. The patent granted was for a process of producing relaxin from a cDNA fragment. One of the grounds upon which it was opposed was that it offends the *ordre public* and morality. Each of the contentions were rejected sequentially:

Tissue sample is to be taken from a pregnant woman and it is an offence against human dignity to make use of a particular female condition (pregnancy) for a technical process oriented towards profit. This was rejected on the basis that the women had given their prior consent for such samples. Moreover, this sample is to be taken only once, after which it could be chemically synthesized.

It amounts to a form of modern slavery since it involves the dismemberment of women and their piecemeal sale to commercial enterprises throughout the world. This infringes the human right to self-determination. This was rejected on the grounds that no right on any individual human being is being granted to the patentee at all.

The patenting of human genes means that human life is being patented, which is intrinsically immoral. This was rejected by pointing out that DNA is not "life" but a substance that carries genetic information. The patenting of a gene has nothing to do with patenting life.

II. NOVELTY

II.1 USA—Inherent and Accidental Anticipation

1. Schering Corp. v. Geneva Pharmaceuticals, Inc., 348 F.3d 992 (Fed. Cir. 2003): Geneva Pharmaceuticals Inc. and other generic drug companies challenged the validity of a Schering patent that claimed descarboethoxyloratadine (DCL), a compound with antihistamine activity. Schering had previously obtained a patent claiming loratadine the active ingredient in an antihistamine drug. In preclinical studies, Schering had determined that DCL was an active metabolite of loratadine (DCL was formed naturally in the body when loratadine was ingested). The contention was raised that prior art loratadine patent inherently anticipated Schering's DCL patent because DCL is a metabolite of loratadine.

The court pointed out that failure to recognize that something had been produced previously does not avoid anticipation if that something was clearly produced. That is, a prior-art reference, silent on a later-claimed compound, can *inherently anticipate* claims to that compound if the *production of the compound necessarily follows* from practicing a process described in the reference. Further, it was clarified that it does not matter that a person skilled in the art may not have recognized that the prior-art process inherently produces the later-claimed compound. Thus, in the case at hand, the metabolite was produced naturally and automatically within the body whenever a person ingested it and the administration of the drug was taught by the prior patent. Therefore, the patent application was held to be inherently anticipated.

2. Tilghman v. Proctor, 102 U.S. 707 (1880): The patent in question involved a process claim for the manufacturing of fatty acids and glycerine from fatty bodies. The process thus described involved mixing the fats with water and maintaining them at a high pressure and temperature.

Prior art had already employed the same process, but in the context of soap-making. Those references treated the fatty acids only as a by-product was never interested in them. The actual process was never really understood. The Supreme Court observed that it would be "*absurd to hold that a patent as anticipated because those skilled in the art later recognize that the discovery was accidentally and unwittingly produced whilst the operators were in pursuit of other and different results, without exciting attention and without its even being known what was done or how it had been done.*" Thus the court opined that the prior art references only accidentally anticipated the invention and are not novelty destroying.

II.2 USA—Utility as Novelty

1. Diamond Rubber Co. of New York v. Consolidated Rubber Tire Co., 220 U.S. 428 (1911): The patent related to an improvement in rubber tires possessing the following elements:

A metallic rim that had flanges configured to from a channel or groove with tapered or inclined sides.

A rubber tire adapted to fit into the channel or groove and of a particular shape.

The location of the fastening or the retaining wires holding the tire to the rim.

The utility of this invention arose from the fact that due to the way the tire was connected to the rim and the shape and configuration of the system, the tire was given the flexibility to be mobile to a certain extent and thus could cushion lateral blows and at the same time not compromise on the firmness with which the tire was held.

The court in this case was considering two prior art patents granted in the United Kingdom. Although both used similar mechanisms of fastening wires, their location was different and they used U or V shaped rims the angle at which the flanges were inclined was not as much as given in the patent in question. After a factual inquiry, the court opined that the angling in the flange gave rise to the utility mentioned and this utility which was absent in prior art, raises a presumption of novelty. Further, the court considered the fact that the person claiming the patent to be invalid had used the patented tire, which was held to further support the novelty of the invention.

2. Parke-Davis & Co. v. H.K. Mulford & Co., 189 F. 95 (C.C.S.D.N.Y. 1911), aff'd in part, 196 F. 496 (2d Cir. 1912): The case related to adrenalin, a substance present naturally in the human body. A researcher working for Mulford had developed a new method of extracting adrenalin from human glands for therapeutic use. The prior art was a patent which had already taught producing adrenalin by drying out the adrenal glands and crushing them into powder. Unlike this prior art, the new process developed by the researcher led to purified adrenalin with lesser impurities and thereby having a better therapeutic effect than the one in the prior art.

The patent holder brought an infringement suit and the suit was resisted on the grounds that this pure form of adrenalin was a new compound, not covered by prior art. The court accepted this argument and held that since the product developed by Mulford was different in the sense of having lesser impurities (different structural association between molecules) and was more therapeutically useful. Thus the purified form was considered as a "new" product and therefore not infringing the patent.

[**Note**: Although the case is not on the 'novelty' requirement *per se*, this case is considered as a landmark one for the holding that a purified form of a known substance that is more useful is a different and new substance for the purposes of patent law.]

3. Merck & Co. v. Olin Mathieson Chemical Corp., 253 F.2d 156 (4th Cir. 1958): Here, the patent in question was directed to vitamin B-12, which was naturally occurring and faced a challenge on the grounds that it was a product of nature and therefore not patentable subject-

matter. The court took an unprecedented approach and held that so long as something can satisfy the statutory requirements of "new and useful" composition of matter, the patent was not to be rejected on the ground that it was naturally occurring as well.

On the question as to whether the claimed compound is "new and useful", the isolated purified form, which was the subject-matter of the patent in question, was held to be new on the basis that the patented composition was of great medicinal and commercial value unlike the natural one. The court held that "*a new and useful product that is the result of processes of extraction, concentration, and purification of natural materials does not defeat its patentability as long as it has a new utility*."

II.3 Europe

1. T 0212/01, Albany International Corp. v. Hoechst Trevira GmbH & Co. KG, 2003: The claim was directed to paper machine clothing made of filaments suitable for use in the forming, pressing or drying sections of a paper making machine. The invention required that the clothing be comprises of a polyester material having a hindered carboxyl group, and having a melting point greater than 260°C. The patent disclosed a preferred polyester for this purpose. An opposition proceeding was initiated on the grounds that the invention lacks novelty and is anticipated.

In evidence, was a public document that dealt with the art of paper making. It also expressly discussed paper machine screens/clothing, along with what fibers can be used for this purpose and the method of treating the said fibers. This document explicitly stated that poly-(1,4-dimethylolcyclohexaneterephthalate), a polyester, can be used for this purpose. Another document evidenced that this polyester had a hindered carboxyl group and a melting point lying between 285°C and 295°C (greater than 260°C. In the opinion of the Board, a person skilled in the field would directly and unambiguously use the information to use filaments of poly-(1,4-dimethylolcyclohexaneterephthalate) in order to produce paper making clothing or screens, which is what is being claimed by the patentee. Therefore, the invention is anticipated. The mere fact that the prior art document indicates other materials which can be used to make the fibers or the fact that it deals with making products other than paper making screens/clothing would not mean that the test for novelty is not satisfied. So long as a person skilled in the art could clearly decipher the invention from the document.

2. T 0782/05, E.I. Du Pont De Nemours And Company v. Degussa GmbH & Ors., 2005: One of the claims in question was directed to a process for manufacturing parts through injection molding, wherein polyamide having an excess of acid or amine end groups such that the number of end groups in excess is at least 2 times the end groups not in excess (ration of 2:1 or above), is injected into the mold. One public document had disclosed the same process in the context of making test plates. A second document disclosed the process to polyamide compositions where the said ratio was 1.9:1 or above and specific examples in the document disclosed those where the ratio was higher than 2:1. It disclosed the use of such unbalanced polyamides to manufacture test bars.

The contention was taken up that the said ratio is adjusted in the invention to control the melt viscosity of the polyamide resin and this use has not been disclosed in any prior art – the so called "use" claims. This was contended to be the technical advancement that would satisfy the novelty ingredient, citing prior decisions of the Board. The Board disagreed and distinguished the cited cases on this basis: whereas *use claims which define the use of a 'particular entity' to achieve an 'effect' are allowed on the basis that it produces a technical effect, use claims which define a use to produce a 'product' are not allowed.* In the instant case, the use of the unbalanced polyamide in the injection molding process results in a 'product' and not producing any 'effect' as such. Such being the case, following the process as disclosed in prior art would inherently or *inevitably* result in the controlling the melt viscosity. Therefore, it was held that prior art has already disclosed the invention and the invention thus lacks novelty.

3. T 0867/93, AEG Hausgeräte GmbH v. Matsushita Refrigeration Company, 1995: Here, the patent was directed to a refrigerator comprising a refrigerator chamber partitioned into two using a partition plate. The lower chamber had a vegetable storage container open at the top with a lid member. The lid member was formed with a humidity permeable film having gas permeability. A cold air convection path was defined between the lid member and the partition plate so as to be communicated with the upper cooling chamber.

A prior patent covered such a refrigerator, but the first embodiment in it did not have the lid member formed with a humidity-permeable film having gas permeability for the vegetable container and no cold air convection path was defined between the lid member and the partition plate. A third embodiment in that patent disclosed these features, but the vegetable container was not the same. The question was can these two embodiments within the same document be combined for the purposes of novelty.

The Board held, citing a prior decision that *different embodiments in a single prior art document may not normally be combined in order to create artificially an embodiment which would destroy novelty of the claimed subject-matter unless the document itself suggests such a combination of features*. On facts, the court held that the prior art document itself nowhere suggested or gave a hint to combine the features of the different embodiments.

III. NON-OBVIOUSNESS

III.1 USA

1. Hotchkiss v. Greenwood, 52 U.S. 248 (1850): A patent was granted for a new and useful improvement in making door and other knobs of all kinds. The invention claimed was directed towards manufacturing knobs of a particular configuration and made of potter's clay, or any kind of clay used in pottery, and shaped and finished by moulding, turning, burning, and glazing, and also made of porcelain. Not even a single element of the system or configuration was claimed to be new. Instead, the only change from what was known in prior art was that unlike prior art which used wood or metal for the knobs, this invention used clay or porcelain.

The court held that although the invention is new in the strict sense, it was not worthy of a patent. The test was that if no more ingenuity and skill was necessary to construct the new knob than was possessed by an ordinary mechanic acquainted with the business then it could not be patented.

2. Graham v. John Deere Co., 383 U.S. 1 (1966): One of the patents in question related to a device designed to absorb shock in plow shanks as they plow through rocky soil, and thus to prevent damage to the plow. The patentee used springs for this purpose. Five prior art patents had already taught the use of springs in plow shanks and in one form or another had all the elements of the invention. The only difference between the invention and the prior art that was pressed was the interchanging of the position of the shank and hinge plate. This allowed the shank to flex under stress for its entire length and thus more effectively absorbs the forces of the shock of obstructions. After laying down the four factor test, the court held that any skilled person who would want the plow shank to more effectively absorb the shock would have contemplated the invention since that was the only other configuration pos-

sible apart from what was already known in prior art. Therefore, any skilled person would have immediately identified the invention and is this obvious.

The other patent in question involved a method of sealing spray cap cover for insecticides. The invention combined a finger-operated pump sprayer, mounted in a container or bottle by means of a container cap, with a plastic overcap which screws over the top of and depresses the sprayer. When the overcap is screwed down, it depresses the sprayer and the pump plunger thereby rendering it inoperable and a seal is formed by the engagement of a circular ridge or rib located above the container's cap. All the elements of the invention except the use of a sealing rib which prevents the contact between the overcap and the container cap, were admitted to be prior art. These features were also available in a prior patent, which related to 'pouring sprouts', whereas the invention in question related to pump sprayers. The court held that problem that was solved by the invention in question was a mechanical closure problem and not limited to the insecticide industry *per se* and therefore the prior art reference on 'pouring spouts' was also relevant. And that patent clearly disclosed the use of a rib and a space between the container cap and the overcap. It was held that anyone skilled in this art would have been aware of this solution proposed in the invention.

3. KSR v. Teleflex, 127 S.Ct. 1727 (2007): The patent in question related to an adjustable (can be positioned according to the comfort of the driver) electronic pedal assembly in automobiles. Position-adjustable pedal system using a fixed pivot point was already patented but that lacked electronic sensors which would convert the mechanical action of pushing the pedal into digital data which was to be fed into a processor that would in turn control the engine throttle. But the use of electronic sensors in pedal assemblies was also known in prior art. Two other patents has separately taught that the sensors could be placed at the pedal's footpad, but which would result in the wearing out of the electronic wires or in the engine compartment, and which would result in damage to the sensors due to the heat and making connections therein were complex. But both these were non-adjustable pedals. Further, there was one more patent on position-adjustable pedals using electronic sensors where the sensors were located at the footpad.

The patentee had essentially combined these patents to have a position-adjustable pedal using electronic sensors which were located at a fixed pivot point (not the engine compartment or the pedal's footpad). The Supreme Court held that the patent was obvious. To the court, the invention was merely a result of common sense since when prior art had already taught that the sensors placed at the footpad or the engine compartment would have disadvantages, the only other location where the sensor could be placed was in the pivot, which is exactly what the patentee did. The court held that a skilled person is presumed to apply common sense as well and that this invention was an advance that would have occurred in ordinary course. The mere fact that there was no *explicit* teaching, suggestion or motivation to combine these references, the court held that the TSM test is flexible and applies even for implied suggestions. The invention was held to be clearly motivated from the nature of the problem to be solved.

III.2 Europe

1. T 24/81, BASF case, 13 October 1982: The claim in this case was directed towards a method for treating melts of pig-iron and steel or steel alloys in a converter, crucible or other vessel, where the oxidizing and the scavenging process was carried out using carbonic acid in one vessel on a continuous basis until the finished steel is produced. The only difference between the invention and the prior art was that the entire process was carried out with gas containing carbon dioxide (from carbonic acid).

Taking the "*problem-solution*" approach, the court held that the applicant wished to solve the following problems:

avoiding an overheating of the melt which necessarily leads to a reduction in the service life of the converter lining and to contamination of the melt with converter particles; and

preventing the formation of red iron-oxide smoke during the oxidising process, in order thereby to dispense with the need for costly filtering equipment.

With respect to the first problem, prior art had already found the use of carbon dioxide oxidising agent since its reaction with the carbon in steel cooled the melt faster. Another prior art document separately disclosed that use of carbon dioxide to solve the second problem as well and that document also disclosed that both problems were associated. Further, another prior art taught that purity could be increased by using a scavenging gas, such as carbon dioxide. Thus any person skilled in the art would have inevitably combined the teachings and is expected to do so. Therefore, the invention lacked inventive step.

2. T 2/83, Rider case, 15 March 1984: The invention related to a tablet that had both anti-flatulency effects combined and antacid effects.

> The tablet used known substances that had this therapeutic effect. The problem with prior art combinations of these two substances was the fact that when simethicone (having anti-flatulency effects) is in intimate contact with an antacid component, its release is delayed or to some extent prevented in consequence of a strong absorption by the antacid bases.

Prior art was replete with use of barriers between the two incompatible components but the trend was to avoid such barriers since they were cumbersome to manufacture. One specific reference taught that a gastro-intestinal formulation can contain silicone oil and a substance which is active in the gastro-intestinal tract, the two agents being separately presented in different volume portions and having barrier means in between. The invention differed from this prior art only in that it employed a specific silicone oil, i.e. simethicone, and an antacid as a gastro-intestinal agent.

A second prior art reference taught that a small amount of simethicone could be reversibly adsorbed on the surface of a suitable carrier that can be mixed with the antacid or can be layered separately within a single tablet. The only difference between the invention and this prior art was in that there was an additional barrier between the layers containing simethicone, on the one hand, and antacid, on the other.

The court held the patent not to be obvious. The court noted that the patentee has, by research, discovered a yet unrecognized problem of migration of simethicone, against all expectations, from the adsorbed state into the solid antacid layer and becomes absorbed therein. The other proposed solution of entrapping the simethicone in a matrix of a suitable carrier was also discovered to be unsatisfactory due to the need to breakdown of matrix itself. Therefore, although a skilled person '*could*' have additionally used a barrier between the layers, in the given facts, he '*would*' not have done so in expectation of some improvement or advantage since the problem had not yet been identified. Till the time of the applicant's disclosure, the second reference was considered by all (commercially) to be an effective solution and thus at that time a skilled person would have deemed a barrier to be superfluous. Thus the invention was not equal to an evitable "one way street" solution and therefore possesses inventive step.

IV. UTILITY/INDUSTRIAL APPLICABILITY

IV.1 USA

1. Brenner v. Manson, 383 U.S. 519 (1966): Manson attempt to obtain a patent on a method of making a steroid that was similar to a known

steroid with tumour-inhibiting properties. The description did not disclose whether the steroid actually worked. The court had to decide whether the application satisfied the test of a 'useful' invention to satisfy the requirements of patentability.

The Supreme Court opined that the object of the requirement of utility was to ensure that the patent monopoly is not too broad thereby does not block off scientific developments since at a later point in time, a skilled person may put to use the invention. Thus by restricting it only those with a specific utility, ultimately public benefit is served. On facts, the court held that the patent at hand does not show any specific utility at all. Although the applicant had shown that a homologue (related compounds differing from one another by a group having one atom of carbon and two atoms of hydrogen a series of such groups) of the compound produced from the process had a specific utility in the form of tumour-inhibiting properties, the description had not proved that the compound itself will have the same property. On the other hand, in view of the inherent unpredictability of the compounds in that filed, a contrary presumption can be drawn. Thus the process was only meant for further research activity having no immediate utility. The mere fact that a process produces a product will not give rise to a utility, unless the product itself can create that utility.

IV.2 Europe

1. T 898/05, ZymoGenetics, Inc. case, 7 July 2006: Here, the invention disclosed a nucleotide sequence and the encoded amino acid sequence of the human transmembrane receptor Zcytor1. Computer-assisted models suggested that it was a member of the hematopoietin receptor family and it was assigned a role in proliferation, differentiation and/or activation of immune cells, a role in early thymocyte development and immune response regulation and a possible role for its ligands in therapeutic conditions associated with the functioning of the immune system. The invention further describes its potential use in different screening methods, in particular to screen for ligands for the receptor, including the natural ligand, as well as agonists and antagonists of the natural ligand. The biological activity of agonist ligands was identified as stimulation of cell-mediated immunity and of lymphocyte proliferation, and that of antagonists as suppression of the immune system.

The objection was taken that the description does not specify any credible use and the use is only vaguely described. Admittedly, no experimental evidence for the suggested role of the receptor and/or its ligands was made available in the application. The court re-iterated the position of law as regards the interpretation of the phrases 'industrial application' and 'industry'. The court noted that in the given facts, prior art indicated that among the members belonging to the hematopoietin receptor family, there was redundancy of action as well as an ability to elicit, under certain conditions, similar biological responses and thus the assigned role to the receptor was credible and prior art supports it. The mere fact that this identification was done through computer models would not changes its credibility especially when not contradicted by prior art. The court also allowed post-grant research thaty confirmed some part of this "educated guess" was taken into evidence to lend support to this conclusion.

As regards the contention that the use is only vaguely described, the court held that for such compounds, their function can be identified as three levels: at the molecular level, at the cellular level and its general biological function. No one of these levels is "more specific" than the other, especially when other levels of activity remain completely unknown or only partially characterized. Since the application describes the general biological function, the description of the use is not vague. The application clearly identifies the area wherein the receptor could be of therapeutic use, i.e. how the properties of this receptor may be exploited practically and this was held to be sufficient to prove it to be susceptible of industrial application.

2. T 870/04, Max-Planck-Gesellschaft zur Förderung der Wissenschaften e.V. case, 11 May 2005: The claim in question related to an isolated, enriched or purified protein and a method of identifying a compound capable of activating or inhibiting the said protein. In laying down a principle of law, the Technical Board of appeals made the following observation:

> "If a function is well known to be essential for human health, then the identification of the substance having this function will immediately suggest a practical application in the case of a disease or condition caused by a deficiency ... In cases where a substance ... is identified ... but either its function is not known or it is complex and incompletely understood, and no disease or condition has yet been identified as being attributable to an excess or deficiency of the substance, and no other practical use is suggested for the substance, then industrial applicability cannot be acknowledged."

On facts, although the specific roles of the protein were identified, the application stops short of suggesting, let alone identifying, an anti-cancer activity or any therapeutic effect. There was no evidence whether it has a positive (promoting and/or supporting tumour growth and/or differentiation) or a negative (tumour-suppressor) one, especially in a complex area such as this. The court held that though the protein could be 'made and used' as a further tool for exploring the complex cellular signal transduction pathways and their implications in the regulation of cellular processes and, possibly, disease states, the the whole burden is left to the reader to guess or find a way to exploit it in industry by carrying out work in search for some practical application geared to financial gain, without any confidence that any practical application exists. Therefore, it was held not to be susceptible of industrial application.

V. ENABLEMENT

1. Enzo Biochem, Inc. v. Calgene, Inc., 14 F. Supp.2d 536 (Del. 1998): The claims at issue were directed to encompass the technology of antisense gene regulation. Antisense technology is based on the insertion into a cell of a sequence of DNA that is the reverse of some portion of the DNA of the target gene; the goal is to suppress the target gene and thus its protein. The patent was being claimed on the basis of three working examples in one bacterium (*E. coli*) with three bacterial genes. But the claim was directed to any cell type, i.e., even those other than the disclosed bacterium. Additionally, expert evidence in the form of testimony and research articles was produced to lend support to the conclusion that this technology was of generic nature and can be applied in other cell types as well.

Based on expert evidence, which indicated that: (a) antisense technology is not so universally known and research was currently pending; and (b) this technology was known to be complicated to apply in a few instances, the court held that the art was inherently unpredictable. The court also noted that the inventor himself had failed in his attempt to use the same technology successfully in five other cell types. Based on this factual inquiry, the court concluded that the claim scope was too broad for the limited enablement provided and thus the patent was held not to fulfill the enablement requirement.

VI. UTILITY/INDUSTRIAL APPLICABILITY

VI.1 Preamble

1. Corning Glass Works v. Sumitomo Elec. U.S.A., Inc., 868 F.2d 1251 (Fed. Cir. 1989): In question was the validity of a patent directed towards an optical waveguide. The claim's preamble or introductory

phrase was "*An optical waveguide* comprising..." The structure as was disclosed in the body of the claim was already disclosed in a previous patent. The party questioning the validity of the patent argued that the patent lacked novelty and was anticipated by this prior patent. As per the law, novelty is destroyed only by a prior art reference that contains all the elements / limitations of the claim. The question then boiled down whether the preamble in the claim in question would amount to a claim limitation, since the use of the disclosed structure as an optical wave guide was not disclosed in the prior patent.

The court held that the there is no litmus test for deciding when the preamble would amount to a claim limitation; it depends upon the patent in its entirety. Borrowing from the specification, the court noted that optical waveguides are unique types of optical fiber, wherein only pre-selected modes of light can propagate and this is in turn dependant upon many structural factors and index of refraction. The patent specification had detailed out the complex equations and worked out the structural requirements etc. that would be required for an optical fiber to act as an optical waveguide. Therefore, in these circumstances, reading the claim in the context of the specification, the court held that the preamble acted as a claim limitation, thereby distinguishing it from the prior patent.

VI.2 Transition Phrases/Connectors

1. AK Steel Corp. v. Sollac, 344 F.3d 1234 (Fed. Cir. 2003): The claims in question were directed to hot-dip aluminium-coated stainless steel. The claim language of one of the patents used the phrase "... the coating metal *consisting essentially of* aluminum ..." For particular scientific (chemical) reasons, the specification disclosed that the silicon contents in aluminium must not exceed 0.5% by weight. The patentee had filed an infringement suit against an infringer who was using aluminium metal with 8–8.5% silicon. The court held that the specification itself discloses the fact that silicon contents more than 0.5% would have a material and negative effect and for this reason, specifically indicated the silicon content requirement. Further, this distinguished the invention from prior art. Since the silicon content requirement materially affected the working of the invention, it is a critical feature of the invention and therefore the claim scope is limited to only aluminium with 0.5% silicon.

19

IPR Strategy and IPR Policy

Intellectual Property is an intangible asset that is now assuming increasing importance. It is used aggressively by many organizations, and sold and traded for monetary and other gains. Acquisition of the proper set of rights to an intellectual property is essential to obtain adequate return on investment. However, being intangible in nature, knowing the adequate value provided by the rights of the intellectual property is also a difficult proposition. But there are increasing efforts towards quantifying the value provided by the obtaining of a intellectual property rights.

IP STRATEGY

Any IP asset ideally goes through three main phases: Generation, Rights Acquisition/Protection, Value Realization. Each of these phases requires considerable amount of investment of resources such as time and money. However such critical resources are generally in short supply, and hence need to be used judiciously. On occasions, the resources may also need to be juggled very creatively to meet the growing demands. Often times, IP assets generated may not go through the entire life-cycle due to various constraints and other reasons.

IP Strategy involves a sustained effort to ensure returns in the investments towards IP assets and these involve any or all forms of intellectual property rights. IP assets are typically in the form of know-how, data, in-house knowledge, and so on. Subsequently, this can be converted into patents, trade-secrets, designs, trademarks, copyrights etc. for various reasons. An organization must have streamlined in-house processes to capture all these different kinds of potential IP assets. These would include notebook policy and invention capture process. A decision has to be made in a timely manner as to the best kind of IP rights protection for the asset generated.

Then, the actual protection is sought by the timely preparation and filing of the necessary documents with the appropriate patent office(s). On many occasions, this involves working closely with external parties such as IP service firms or law firms. Of course, the protection of knowledge through careful use of trade secrets cannot be underestimated. In the information age, knowledge is power, and thus, knowing a bit of information that a competition does not know gives power in the marketplace. However, the person formulating and implementing an IP strategy must also be fully aware of the limitations of trade secrets. Any kind of trade secret can be reverse engineered or acquired through diligent research or through any other legitimate means available to any of the competitors.

IP generation requires, at the very least, time commitment, and very often, the use of resources. Some technology domains like chemistry and pharmaceuticals require infrastructure and other materials that are generally quite expensive. Thus, one must be aware of success and possible failures while attempting to generate IP assets. Considerable time, resources and effort can be saved by having a thorough search and analysis done ahead of time. Typically, research efforts in an organization are focused based on core competency and identifying critical and desirable market needs. Subsequently, a good research program would also include a thorough (or as comprehensive as possible) landscape analysis. A clear knowledge of the players in the field, the key patents held by others, who are the competitors and other bits of information is a useful place to start. Then, competitor-watch, patent-watch etc., can be done periodically to keep abreast of developments. Once this is done, a clearer picture emerges that enables one to make an informed decision regarding the research program and some outcomes of it can be arrived at. At this point, one can formulate a strategy that provides guidelines for focusing research efforts, defines timelines, gives a fair idea of the kind of IP assets to be generated and product(s) that can be made and sold without infringing on others' rights.

All applications towards the registration of an IP right, including, patent, trademark, design etc., must be carefully drafted and reviewed. A patent application must be carefully scrutinized, with special attention to be given to claimed subject matter versus disclosed matter. The patent application must also be reviewed for whether it is in line with the original IP strategy. Further, all those involved in the generation and protection of IP assets must also be fully aware of any other related work, and data and results from that, so that each filed application covers only relevant data and does not create a barrier for future applications, while still obtaining the adequate protection it deserves.

A patent provides the right to exclude others from making, selling, using or importing without the owner(s)' prior permission. Once this exclusivity is obtained, patents can be used to generate revenue. Patents may be filed to protect one or more product, or components of the product. After a determination has been made that a product does not infringe on other's rights, the said product or component can be made or sold. In this way, the value of the patent is directly realized. However, patents may also be filed merely to prevent others from practising an invention. In such instances, the patents may be used to generate revenue through other means. This may be achieved by careful policing the market place and filing lawsuits against blatant infringers, and making them pay for wrongfully cutting into the real owner's marketshare.

Patents, like other assets, can be sold and traded for monetary returns. This kind of transaction can be in various forms.

Selling or Assigning is when ownership of the patents permanently transferred to another entity in exchange for an agreed-upon payment once or other considerations, with no future royalties. In this case, the value of a patent is obtained immediately. This transaction is preferred for technologies that run the risk of being superseded by another technology before the value of the patent can be fully realized.

Licensing of patents is done to realize its value through royalties for the remainder of the life of the patent. The value is obtained through slow incremental amounts over a longer time period. This kind of transaction is particularly useful when the owner of a patent is not in a position to make a product: (a) at all, (b) in sufficient quantity to meet a given market need, or (c) to cover a given geographical area.

Licensing can further be of different types:

Sole Licence is a situation wherein only a single person or entity is given a licence to practise the invention. In this case the licensee and the patent owner have the right to use the patented technology.

Exclusive Licence is a situation wherein only a single person or entity is given a licence to practise the invention. In this case, however, only the licensee has the right to use the patented technology, which cannot even be used by the patent owner.

Non-Exclusive Licence is a situation wherein several parties are given licence to practise the invention, thus all licensees and the patent owner have the right to use the patented technology.

Cross Licence is a situation where two or more organizations license patents to each other in order to consolidate respective market positions.

VALUATION

The price for which a patent is sold or the nature of returns from a barter-type licensing agreement is to be determined based on several factors. Some of the factors that determine the value of a patent include market size, amount of prior art, term remaining on the patent, significance of the patent in terms of whether it is a breakthrough or incremental, whether it contributes to a strong brand name (trademark), number of prior art owned by the owner of the patent in question versus those owned by others, and so on. A few simple methods to determine the value of a patent are as follows:

Transaction method: This involves calculating the actual price paid for a similar intangible product or service under similar circumstances.

Income method: This is the most commonly used patent valuation method. The method focuses on the expected income stream that the patent holder would get during the lifetime of the patent.

Replacement cost method: This method establishes the value of the patent by calculating the cost of developing a similar asset either internally or externally.

Market method: The value of a patent is assessed based on the value of comparable transactions made in the market.

Option-based methods: In this case, the value is estimated based on the option pricing methods. This method was initially developed for use in pricing stock options.

Other methods using probabilistic estimates include Real Option method, Monte Carlo simulations, Binomial Expansion method, etc.

Knowing what to expect in terms of monetary returns and actively seeking ways to realize it forms an important part of IP strategy. IP strategy also involves decisions regarding one's positions towards competition – passive or aggressive. Decisions such as opposing or invalidating dominating patents that may otherwise render a product as infringing need to be made. Even the invalidation proceedings can take the shape of an *inter parte* or *ex parte* proceedings in US, depending on the initial actions. Similarly, infringers have to be identified and if found, the nature of actions against them have to be determined. Such actions may include negotiation for royalties or full-blown legal action, or even a private out-of-court settlement. Also, before the launch of any product, a determination has to be made that either the product or any of its components do not infringe anyone else's rights. All these decisions cannot be made without the counseling of IP personnel, who in turn cannot provide proper counsel without adequate data, in other words, a proper search and analysis.

IP strategy also involves decisions regarding maintenance of patents, and managing the portfolio of patents owned by an organization. Since, maintenance of patents involves a cost, periodically one has to check if it is really worth paying the price to maintain a patent. To this end, it is very essential to conduct periodic IP audits. This activity will immediately bring to light all the available patents, and which ones contribute to what extent. The original IP strategy formulated may be used as a benchmark to see if the patents are providing sufficient returns on investments. Wherever the patents have not performed up to the initially expected levels, reasons for its underachievement have to be determined. The learnings gleaned from this can then be used as guidelines for the formulation of all future strategies. A direct outcome of conducting an IP audit includes a decision to maintain or abandon a patent. Abandonment can be achieved by simple non-payment of maintenance fees, or in other words, inactivity.

Further, an effective strategy must also try to work the different forms of IPR in conjunction to meet the business needs and enhance market presence and even ensure market dominance. All the forms of IPR expire at the end of a certain time period, after which whatever was protected is available for the public to utilize. Figure 12 gives an idea as to the maximum time limits allowed for each form of IPR.

Since, trademarks potentially last forever, it is possibly the most powerful form of IPR in terms of ensuring dominance in the marketplace over all the competitors. Thus, carefully orchestrating the use of trademarks when the exclusivity through other forms of IPR such as patents and designs are still active, will be most ideal, because once the exclusivity period expires, the trademarks will remain, and thus, despite the presence of competition in the market, the brand association will carry through during these times.

Thus, formulating an IP strategy is a very important exercise which when done early and properly, can lead to a strong position in the market. Subsequently, this position can be used judiciously to increase bottomlines for the organization. This is a cyclic process wherein the IP strategy is formulated at the beginning, following which it is refined to align with business and technical changes, and once enforced, it is reformulated for a new business and technical demand.

IPR POLICY

In the context of open-innovation, there is an ever-increasing drive for organizations not to rely on own research, but instead to look outside of oneself for productivity, innovation, new ideas, product designs etc. Thus, there has been a significant rise in cooperative research, which may manifest itself as contract research assignments, consultancy, sponsored research & develop-

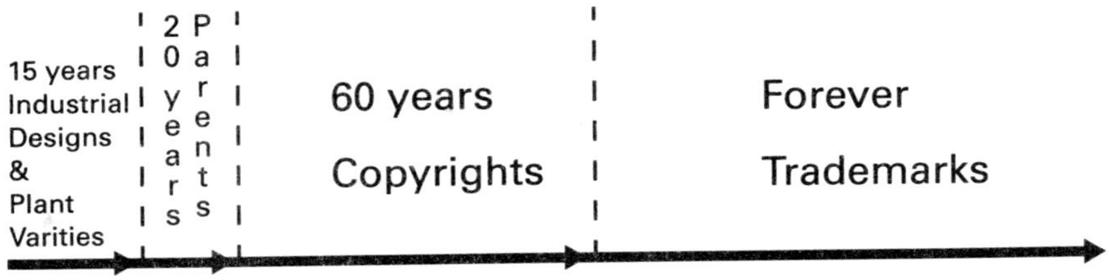

*: Maximum time. From the appropriate starting date & upon proper maintenance

Figure 12. Line diagram depicting the maximum time limits allowed for each form of IPR.

ment activities, and so on, that may include multi-disciplinary teams comprising professionals from within university and industry. Such collaboration results in easy accessibility and efficient utilization of world-class research resources and the best of human minds to interested organizations. Institutions that are part of such collaborations also tend to benefit in that students, researchers and faculty are exposed to the realities of business and markets.

Symbiotic relationships between different organizations can occur only if there are clearly defined, previously agreed upon rules of engagement between them, so that no future animosity or "bad blood" results. A clear, cogent and transparent framework for freely sharing their respective knowledge, information and resources with each other, and defining the "ownership" of the new or original knowledge so that it will culminate in benefits resulting from the commercial or business application being shared in a fair manner ought to be the main focus of any agreement. Thus, an organization's IPR policy must be drafted and implemented such that an environment may be created to meet all the above-mentioned needs. This is of utmost importance, and indeed, a dire necessity in today's environment.

Any IPR-related policy should set forth transparent guidelines for the identification, procurement, incentivization, ownership, protection and commercialization of the Intellectual Property (IP) developed. This will result in the rapid and effective transfer of technology from the laboratory to market and business for maximizing value realization of their creative and innovative output.

Before bringing any third party into the fold for research, development, collaborative or consulting activities, a proper agreement must be put in place that generally agrees with the organizational IPR policy. In turn, an organizational IPR policy must be all-encompassing, and must address all possible situations, including exceptional cases. Subsequently, the IPR policy must constantly be reviewed to ensure that it is keeping up with any organizational changes, if any. The IPR policy must also be applicable to all employees in the organization, regardless of the nature of activity. Thus, it must be broad in its scope.

TYPICAL FEATURES OF AN IPR POLICY

Ownership

The criteria for establishing ownership for all the knowledge and IP generated must be laid down clearly. Various situations have to be envisioned and illustrated here. For instance, in the case of a sponsored research, the rights to all knowledge may be owned by the sponsor, whereas, in a collaborative research and development project, sharing of ownership may be worked out. In the situation where IP is generated through internal funding, the organization should own the rights to it. Employee agreements and contracts must be drafted to proactively obtain this right. This must then be followed up by the execution of appropriate paperwork to assign the ownership rights to each individual IP generated, as per the local law.

The knowledge generated in the process must be assimilated as organizational knowledge and must not be allowed to be lost with the loss of one or more employees. This is very important so resources are not wasted, and prevent reinventing the wheel. Adequate measures must be taken, and this may include measures such as ensuring everyone works in a team, documentation and review of all documents, results, data etc.

In some instances, especially in university and research institution kind of setups, the ownership may also be decided to be given to the inventor or creator. That is to say that the ownership rights that are vested with the institution or university may be given back completely to the one who generated the IP, which may be a faculty, researcher, student, professor etc. However, in such instances, the university or institution may decide that it shall retain a non-exclusive, free of charge, and an irrevocable licence to copy or use the work for its own purpose.

Confidentiality

Typically, all information and knowledge within an organization must be regarded as confidential and all measures must be taken to protect it. This includes constantly reminding the employees about the confidentiality and its importance. Employee contracts must also include a confidentiality clause. A good process must also be in place that will review any data and information before publishing articles or in a conference. Any involvement of third party must be preceded by a confidentiality prior to the start of any discussions or negotiations.

Nature of Agreements

A good IPR policy will also delineate the nature of agreement to be drafted whenever the involvement of a third party becomes necessary. This can be streamlined by the use of third-party involvement form, wherein the details of the third party, nature of services expected, the nature of information exchanged, reasons for their involvement etc., can be given. Subsequently, the agreement can be drafted addressing all these points. Further these details will also help in drafting the clauses concerning ownership of rights on any IP generated, confidentiality, benefits sharing, and other such points. Agreements may also contain standard clauses such as force majeure, arbitration mediation, dispute resolution, and so on.

Invention Capture Document

Any IP generated must be captured as early as possible. This may be facilitated by the use of an Invention Capture Document, wherein all the details related to the invention should be collected. This includes all the relevant prior art, the nature of the invention such as the problem being addressed, the solutions posed earlier, the current solution which clearly differentiates from the prior art, inventorship, and so on.

The Invention Capture Document will be used to determine whether the invention needs to be protected. This determination will be made by a review of a team of experts formed from the IPR Cell, which structure will be discussed in the following section. The outcome of the review may be several-fold: the invention may be filed for protection as such, more data may be required before further review, the invention may not be worth protecting, etc., The reviewing team should have clear guidelines for the evaluation. The IP Strategy may be consulted to make this determination. Once a decision towards the outcome of the invention has been arrived at, it must be clearly communicated to the inventors. At this point, the IP Strategy may also be used to determine the nature of protection, the jurisdictions for which the protection is sought, the resources required for obtaining, and all other considerations. Any involvement of outside counsel for filings must be preceded by the appropriate engagement letters and confidentiality agreements.

Incentives

Inventors may be given bonus in many ways to promote the culture of innovation. This may be monetary in nature, or other forms of incentives may also be given to keep the spirits and morale up. The incentives should be such that others in the team and the organization are inspired to achieve the same, while making it worthwhile for the inventor to have gone through the ardour of inventing. Given the importance, this section of IPR Policy needs to be formulated with extreme care and transparency.

IPR Policy must also provide guidance for the audit of the IPR awareness among employees, and must ensure the IP compliance of everyone in this organization with no exception. The simple clause that 'ignorance is not a defense or an excuse' must be drilled into all the employees, and should also be extended to contractors, vendors, and all those associated with the organization. The policy must indicate the consequences of non-compliance, including disciplinary/punitive actions, if any.

To achieve consistency in the understanding and interpretation of the professional and legal terminology especially related to IPR, the IPR Policy should provide a glossary of all the relevant terms. Further, to make the IPR Policy document user-friendly, illustrations using typical examples so that all potential users of the policy are able to relate to its provisions in a practical manner may also be done.

IPR Team

One of the most important aspects of an IPR Policy is the availability of an IPR Team. The process of policy formulation is best initiated with the formation of a formal cross-functional core team of researchers, development team, marketing team, business managers, in-house IPR professionals, and other relevant members to identify and address:

- all issues concerning the creation and exploitation of intellectual assets,
- avenues for interacting with the external world through appropriate contracts and agreements,
- identification and disclosure of intellectual assets,
- joint research results ownership, their subsequent commercialization, and revenue sharing,
- valuation of intellectual assets,
- technology transfer,
- resolution of possible conflict of interest,
- avoid infringement of IP of others, and consequent damages, liabilities, etc.

The importance of an IP Team towards an organization will be felt throughout when it accomplishes the following:

- facilitate systematic, timely development and utilization of IPR assets; promote the harmonious development of IPR policy; and
- provide guidance, support and appropriate expert resources for identification, protection, use, management and transfer of IPR assets.

To meet the goals defined, the IPR Team must be involved in activities that include:

- creating awareness of the importance and role of IPR;

- defining the rights and responsibilities of all involved and communicating to the entire organization;
- ensuring transparency and fairness of the IPR policy to encourage compliance and solicit feedback regarding the fulfilment of the objectives of the IPR policy; and
- instituting a review mechanism of the policy for fine-tuning and improvement to ensure "relevance" of the policy to the changing environment and evolving needs.

Often times, due to stressed resources inside an organization, the IPR Team may be a one person team, who is working with a loose group of individuals and several outside consultants and vendors, as part of the "Team". This situation also works quite effectively as long as the roles and responsibilities of each of this extended team is clearly well-defined and ownership issues and quality-related matters have been sorted out early on during the relationship with external parties.

Implementing an effective IPR Strategy along with a robust IPR Policy is a great necessity in today's global "open" world where everybody does a little bit of something that contributes to a final outcome. This final outcome is usually in the form of an effective product or an efficient service that is offered to customers at a premium price. Without such a vision and a policy in place, things might happen in ad-hoc manner, which means the success becomes a matter of probability. To ensure reproducible success, a smooth and well-conceived plan must be in place ahead of time, which is then executed with precision and accuracy. IPR is but a tool, albeit an effective one, in the hands of a deft operator skilled in excluding others from one's own piece of pie.

Bibliography

1. Indian Patents Act and Patent Rules: www.ipindia.nic.in and follow links from there to the latest versions and amendments.
2. Manual of Patent Practice & Procedure, Intellectual Property India: www.ipindia.nic.in and follow links from there to the latest versions and amendments.
3. Copyright Act of India: http://copyright.gov.in/
4. SICLD Act, India: http://www.mit.gov.in/default.aspx?id=317
5. Trademarks Act, India: www.ipindia.nic.in and click on trademarks link
6. Design Act, India: www.ipindia.nic.in and click on the Designs link
7. Plant Varieties Protection & Farmers' Variety Act, India: www.plant authority.in/
8. Code of Federal Regulations (CFR), USA: http://www.uspto.gov/web/patents/legis.htm
9. Manual of Patent Examination Procedure, USPTO: http://www.uspto.gov/web/patents/legis.htm
10. European Patent Convention & EPC Guidelines: http://www.epo.org/patents/law/legal-texts/epc.html
11. Intellectual Property for Business Series Number 1: Making a Mark: An Introduction to Trademarks for Small and Medium-Sized Enterprises, WIPO Publication No. 900.
12. Intellectual Property for Business Series Number 2: Looking Good: An Introduction to Industrial Designs for Small and Medium-Sized Enterprises, WIPO Publication No. 498.
13. Intellectual Property for Business Series Number 3: Inventing the Future: An Introduction to Patent for Small and Medium-Sized Enterprises, WIPO Publication No. 917.

14. Intellectual Property for Business Series Number 4: Creative Expression: An Introduction to Copyright and Related Rights for Small and Medium-Sized Enterprises, WIPO Publication No. 918.
15. Intellectual Property: A Power Tool for Economic Growth by Kamil Idris, WIPO Publication No. 888.1.
16. Secrets of Intellectual Property: A Guide for Small and Medium-Sized Exporters, a Publication by International Trade Centre UNCTAD/WTO and WIPO, 2004.
17. Marketing Crafts and Visual Arts: The Role of Intellectual Property. A Practical Guide, a Publication by International Trade Centre UNCTAD/WTO and WIPO, 2003.
18. Intellectual Property Rights: Unleashing the Knowledge Economy by Prabuddha Ganguli; TATA McGraw-Hill Publishing Company (January 2001).
19. Principles of Intellectual Property by Gary Myers; West Publishing Company (July 2008).
20. Mechanics of Patent Claim Drafting by John L. Landis, Practising Law Institute; 2nd edition (1978)
21. How to Write a Patent Application by Jeffrey G. Sheldon, Practising Law Institute (PLI) (December 1, 1992)
22. Principles of Patent Law: Cases and Materials (University Casebook Series) by Donald S. Chisum (Author), Craig Allen Nard (Author), Herbert F. Schwartz (Author), Pauline Newman (Author), F. Scott Kieff (Author), Foundation Press (July 8, 2004)
23. Patent searching : tools and techniques edited by David Hunt, Long Nguyen, and Matthew Rodgers, Wiley, Feb 2, 2007.
24. Patent Searching Made Easy by David Hitchcock, NOLO publishers, 2000.

Index